# Color
# by
# Design

**PAINT AND PRINT WITH DYE**

## ANN JOHNSTON

ANN JOHNSTON, PUBLISHER
LAKE OSWEGO, OREGON
USA

## DEDICATION

To my students all around the world

*Color by Design: Paint and Print with Dye*
© 2001 Ann Johnston
First printing 2001

Library of Congress Control Number 2001 126190

ISBN # 0-9656776-1-3

Published by
Ann Johnston
P. O. Box 944
Lake Oswego, OR 97034
www.annjohnston.net

## CREDITS

Book and cover design by Ann Marra
Editorial assistance by Anne Knudsen
Photography by Bill Bachhuber
Cover photography by City Imaging
Printed in Hong Kong through Global Interprint

## OTHER BOOKS BY ANN JOHNSTON

*The Quilter's Book of Design,* 2000
*Color by Accident: Low-Water Immersion Dyeing,* 1997
*Dye Painting!,* 1992

## ACKNOWLEDGEMENTS

Jim Johnston, Scott and Tod Johnston, Don Wiener, Elin Noble, Ann Poe, Cynthia Corbin, Jeannette Meyer, Elaine Spence, Joan Helm, Chris Vietmeier

Inside front cover:
Yellow, red, and blue sprayed onto dry cotton hanging from clothesline.

Page 1:
Thick black dye brushed and drawn onto dry cotton; later low-water immersion dyed with gold and orange.

Previous page:
Monoprint on dry silk; later low-water immersion dyed with gold and red.

# contents

Dyers are not subject to the season of the year, the region of the world, or current fashions for choices in fabric colors. We have control – over color, value, texture, and pattern – to create fabrics uniquely our own. Learning to dye is particularly rewarding for the artist who wishes to use fabric, because the dyeing process itself is a source of inspiration for further work. My earlier book, *Color by Accident: Low-Water Immersion Dyeing,* teaches an easy method of combining dye, water, and fabric in containers. *Color by Design: Paint and Print with Dye* teaches how to use the same dyes in surface applications on a table. It explains how the dyes can be used with traditional surface design techniques, as well as with some new approaches.

*Color by Design* is a practical guide to exploring color and design directly on fabric. It allows dyers to focus more on color and design than on chemistry. A dyer can get to work at a moment's notice: the fabric, dyes, and other chemicals can be prepared ahead so they are ready to use. The colors are fixed simply by keeping the fabric at room temperature. The colors in the photographs demonstrate the effectiveness of this dye method – all the fabrics have been thoroughly washed unless noted otherwise. Exercises progress from simple to complex and include a wide variety of options for more experienced dyers. Relevant technical details are included for advanced dyers as well. Keep in mind that dyeing is a process with many variables that can change the results. As with everything else, experience makes the process easier, the tools more accurate, and the results more predictable.

# HOW TO USE THIS BOOK

*Color by Design* teaches how to paint and print with dye by giving step-by-step instructions. If you don't do the steps, you won't fully understand an essential part of the process: how the dye looks and spreads when different tools are used. Nor will you learn how to prepare the dye in different consistencies so it will flow or stay put. The more fabric you dye, the more you will learn.

Thickened colors monoprinted from work surface onto dry cotton.

I suggest you begin by reading Chapter 1, *Supplies,* and Chapter 2, *Instructions,* carefully. Then skim through the rest of the book to find out what is there. Next, prepare the dyes, fabric, and auxiliaries following the directions in Chapter 2. These recipes are designed to be easy to use and versatile; they do not require precision measuring instruments, only measuring spoons and cups. If you are a complete beginner, start painting with the first exercise in Chapter 3, *Color Mixing.* If you already know how to mix black and gray, as well as all the colors you like, start with Chapter 4, *Moisture Variations.* You should be thoroughly aware of all the variations of wet and dry fabric and thick and thin colors before you go on to Chapter 5, *Paint Techniques.*

The early exercises in the book explain every detail in the process. As you progress through the chapters, I have assumed that you no longer need basic instructions to be repeated. Where amounts are given, they are suggestions to give you an idea of how much to prepare. Where an amount is not suggested, any amount will work to demonstrate the point of the exercise.

As you begin, the most important thing to remember is to have fun. Paint and print and find out what happens. When you're finished, cure and wash the fabric according to the directions in Chapter 2. You'll find that you learn more about color and design with every piece of fabric you dye. —*Ann*

# Learn the Basics

*Color by Design* uses Procion®MX fiber-reactive dyes for natural fibers – cotton, viscose rayon, linen, and silk. The dyes produce a full range of bright hues that mix well. They are easy to use, economical, and resist fading in water and light. The molecules in fiber-reactive dye chemically react with the fiber molecules they contact, resulting in a strong chemical bond. The surface qualities of the dyed fabric, such as texture and luster, are the same after the final washing as before dyeing.

Direct application of the dye to the fabric allows many options, including very fine lines, smooth color gradations and shading, and shapes with or without outlines. To achieve desired effects, colors can be made thick like a gel or thin like water and can be applied to wet or dry fabric, so a dyer can control the flow of dye on the fabric. The final effect can be soft and blurry or precise with hard edges. Dyed colors are transparent, not opaque, so when the dye is applied in layers one design shows through another – one color visually mixes with the color beneath it.

Blue painted on dry cotton with sponge brush and roller, orange stamped with triangular sponge and black drawn with pointed bottle.

# SUPPLIES

You can start dyeing fabric with a minimum amount of equipment at minimal cost. The supplies needed will have to be gathered from different sources, depending on where you live. It is simplest and usually most economical to purchase dye and related chemicals from the businesses that specialize in them (see *Sources* on page 164).

Some items such as palettes and brushes can be found at art supply stores. Look for a suitable work surface and other useful tools at a local hardware store, paint supply, or lumber yard.

Fabric is the most important variable when working with any dye. At first, buy it in small quantities until you know it dyes well, or get it directly from businesses that know the fiber content and any treatments on the fabric. Many of the exercises are on small pieces of fabric, called *fat quarters* because a long narrow quarter of a yard (meter) will tangle in the wash. Four *fat quarters* come from a yard (meter) divided vertically and horizontally into four equal pieces. Each measures approximately 18″ x 22″ (45 cm x 55 cm), depending on the width of the fabric.

From top:
sand weave cotton,
cotton flannel,
cotton printed
with white paint,
cotton twill stripe,
cotton print cloth,
cotton broadcloth,
cotton sateen,
rayon satin, linen,
textured silk,
silk broadcloth,
silk shantung,
silk noil, patterned-
weave silk.

## PROCION®MX COLORS

Procion®MX dye powders are available in over a hundred colors. Most are mixed from fewer than 20 dye powders, called single-chemical colors. The colors produced by the manufacturer are assigned a code which starts with the word Procion, followed by the color name and a number/letter combination used to describe the color. Suppliers who buy large quantities of Procion®MX dye from the manufacturer and repackage them in smaller quantities for studio dyers usually put their own product numbers and names on the colors they sell. Your supplier should provide you with the manufacturer's code. Use the Procion®MX codes I have listed to find the colors I recommend.

There are many more colors available than the single-chemical colors. Some that have a Procion®MX code number are actually mixtures produced by the manufacturer and sold to the industry and dye suppliers. Others are mixed after they have left the factory and do not have a Procion®MX code. I did not include any pre-mixed dye colors, because I find it simpler and more economical to buy only single-chemical colors and mix my own colors after I have prepared liquid dye concentrates from powders. The main exception I make is for black. I buy the manufacturer's black mix, Procion®Black MX-CWNA, and other blacks mixed by dye suppliers.

The manufacturer's codes of the colors I recommend you start with are listed here, along with three suppliers' product numbers. Be sure you are buying Procion®MX dyes that react at room temperature, and not Procion®H dyes that require more heat and/or stronger alkali to fix the colors.

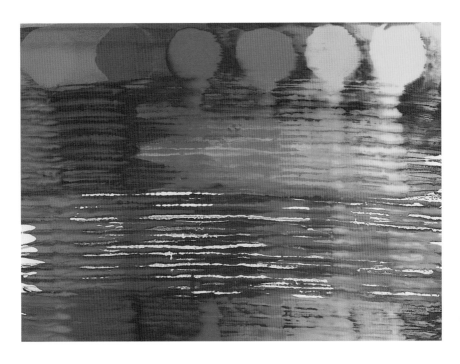

## COLOR LIST FOR EXERCISES

| PROCION®MX CODE | DHARMA TRADING | PRO CHEMICAL | QUILT UND ART | |
|---|---|---|---|---|
| Yellow MX-8G | 1 | 108 | Citrus Yellow | Turquoise MX-G, Blue MX-G, Red MX-8B, Red MX- 5B, Yellow MX-3RA, and Yellow MX-8G monoprinted on dry cotton. |
| Yellow MX-3RA | 4 | 104 | Yellow Orange | |
| Red MX-5B | 12 | 305 | Magenta Red | |
| Red MX-8B | 13 | 308 | Pink Red | |
| Blue MX-G | 23 | 406 | Primary Blue | |
| Turquoise MX-G | 25 | 410 | Turquoise | |
| Black MX-CWNA | *300 | *608 | | |

*All blacks are mixes; use any you prefer.

## MORE SINGLE-CHEMICAL COLORS

Mixing colors with Yellow MX-8G, Red MX-8B, and Blue MX-G
will produce a very wide range of hues. It is not difficult to
remember how to mix a color if you know it is some mixture of
these three dyes. A dark gold-yellow dye, of course, will produce
different mixed colors than a bright yellow dye.

These thickened
colors are painted
on cotton, left and
silk, right.

Yellow MX-8G

Yellow MX-4G

Yellow MX-GR

Yellow MX-3RA

Orange MX-G

Orange MX-2R

Brown MX-GRN

Red MX-5B

Red MX-8B

Brown MX-5BR

Violet MX-G

Blue MX-R

Blue MX-7RX

Blue MX-G

Blue MX-2G

Blue MX-4GD

Turquoise MX-G

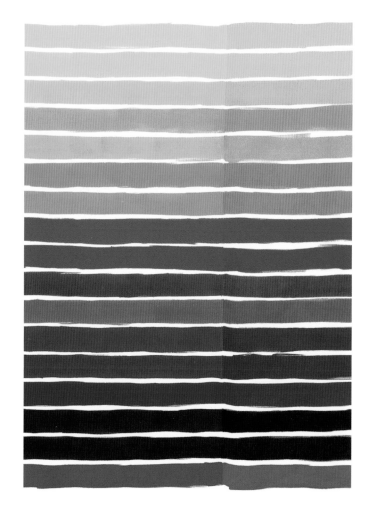

That is why I recommend also buying Yellow M-3RA, Red MX-5B, and Turquoise MX-G to start with. Once you have experimented with these six colors by doing the 48 exercises in *Color by Design,* you will be ready to use more single-chemical colors to produce an even more subtle variety in your palette.

The ownership of the registration of Procion®MX dyes can affect their availability from country to country and from year to year. Not all of the single-chemical colors are carried by all suppliers. Some of them are difficult to find because they are not widely used. The 17 single-chemical colors shown in the photo are the ones I have used to dye fabric.

## AUXILIARY CHEMICALS

### LUDIGOL

Ludigol is the trade name for sodium salt of m-nitrobenzene sulfonic acid, or resist salts L. It is an optional ingredient in the print paste you will use with Procion®MX dyes (page 29), and is suited for use in such locations as highly polluted cities, that have many gasses in the air. The site on the dye molecule that attaches to the fiber can be reduced, or used, by the gasses in the air, making the site unreactive. Ludigol prevents this by combining with the gas, allowing more dye to fix on the fiber.

### METAPHOS

Metaphos is the trade name of sodium hexametaphosphate, a water softener. It is used in print paste (page 29) to make sodium alginate (page 18) flow more smoothly. It does not affect the dye-fiber reaction.

## SODA ASH

Sodium carbonate ($Na_2CO_3$) is the chemical name for soda ash. It allows Procion®MX dye and fiber to make a permanent bond. It makes the water alkaline, and is about the strength of most laundry detergents. Use 100 percent sodium carbonate. Do not confuse it with sodium bicarbonate (baking soda), which is a weaker alkali and will not give the same results. Soda ash very quickly causes dye to bond with fabric or with the water in a mixture. Avoid using old color mixtures that have been contaminated with soda ash solution, because even though they will stain the fabric, the fabric will not be light- or wash-fast.

## SODIUM ALGINATE

Sodium alginate is extracted from seaweed and acts as an antimigrant when mixed with Procion®MX dye. The granules absorb water and swell up without cooking to create a gel that looks lumpy or granular at first, but becomes completely smooth and transparent when the granules are all dissolved (page 29). It keeps the dye from spreading on the fabric the way a plain water solution does, enabling dyers to make designs with distinct edges. Alginate can be used in varying amounts in order to achieve the viscosity required: extra-thick for silk screen work, thinner for fine line painting.

Sodium alginate is available in different grades and viscosities and under different trade names. Sodium alginate SH is the thickener used in all the dye techniques shown in this book, on both cotton and silk. It has low-solid content and high viscosity. It has larger granules and thickens more solution than the other type, sodium alginate F, which has high-solid content and low viscosity. If you are an experienced dyer, you may wish to use both SH and F or a mixture, depending on the application. You may also find sodium alginate sold under the names Keltex, Lamitex, and Manutex.

## SYNTHRAPOL SP

Synthrapol SP is a concentrated surface-active agent used with fiber-reactive dye. It can be used to remove sizing from fabric before dyeing (page 28). After dyeing, any excess dye that has not bonded still has an affinity for the fibers, so a strong agent is needed to penetrate and remove it. Synthrapol is specifically formulated to do this. During the final washing process (page 34), it acts as a surfactant, keeping the unreacted dye in suspension and lessening the chance of staining or transfer.

Where Synthrapol or a similar product is not available, use a detergent that is not alkaline, because alkali is a fixative for the dye. Be sure your detergent is free of bleaching agents.

## UREA

Chemically formulated urea is used to maintain the moisture required for the dye and fiber reaction to occur. It is a common ingredient in household products such as fertilizer and cosmetics. As an ingredient in the print paste used to thicken the dye concentrates (page 29), it acts as a humectant, drawing moisture into the solution. It is especially important in situations where the surface of fabric may dry too quickly. As an ingredient in the dye concentrate (page 30), urea allows more dye powder to dissolve in the water, producing a stronger concentration and thus more saturated colors in the final dyed fabric.

## WATER

Very little water is used with surface applications of dye, so it is not a major factor in the results achieved. There are so many other variables that change the results that the differences in water are hard to detect. If your tap water is extremely hard, i.e. full of minerals, it may be difficult to dissolve the chemicals and you may wish to use filtered or softened water. I have used hard and soft water, from springs, rivers, and wells, without a problem.

## SAFETY TIPS

Procion®MX dyes are versatile and simple to use. Like all the chemicals we use in our daily lives, the dyes and their auxiliaries should be handled with good work standards. Minimizing your exposure to all chemicals makes good sense.

- Avoid breathing dye powder. When measuring powders use dust/mist mask or respirator recommended by dye suppliers. Avoid excessive stirring of powders when measuring, and *always keep lid on powdered dye.*

- Avoid contact with skin and eyes by using gloves and goggles when handling all powdered chemicals.

- Separate dye activities from food preparation. Use separate measuring tools, containers, and storage spaces. Keep all containers labeled and away from children.

- Clean up as you work.

- Request Material Safety Data Sheets prepared for industrial users of dye from manufacturers. Keep up-to-date on recent research.

## FABRIC

The fabric you use for dye painting and printing will determine the results you achieve. Procion®MX dyes are designed to work with plant (cellulose) fibers, primarily cotton, linen, and viscose rayon. They will also work on silk, a protein fiber, because of its molecular structure. They will not dye synthetic fibers. There are many weights and weaves of fabric to choose from, such as muslin, twill, canvas, velvet, corduroy, organza, jersey knits, and sateen. You should consider the following factors when you buy your fabric.

## FIBER TYPE

Each fiber has different qualities that determine how it dyes, so you will see different results depending on the type of fiber. Silk, in particular, results in visibly different colors from cotton. Fabrics that are a mix of natural fibers or a mix of natural and synthetic can give dramatic results.

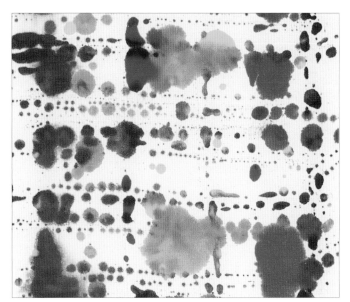

Monoprinted silk noil. The colors appear slightly different and flow very differently on a heavy, nubby cream-colored silk than they would on a smooth, lightweight, bleached white cotton.

## LUSTER

The more reflective the fiber, the darker the colors appear. Mercerized cotton has been treated with caustic alkali in a process that rounds out the fibers and increases the luster as well as the fabric's strength and affinity for dye. It appears about 25 percent darker than the same fabric unmercerized. Cotton can also be causticized, another alkali treatment, which also increases luster and affinity for dye.

## FINISHING TREATMENTS

Untreated fabric is known as greige. Most often, the fabric we buy has been put through a variety of processes. If you buy fabric that has been bleached white, it will dye clearer colors than unbleached, yellowish fabric. If it has been sized with starch to make it crisp, the dye will not penetrate as well. The sizing can be washed off in hot water and detergent (page 28). Some fabric is labeled PFD (prepared for dyeing) or PFP (prepared for printing), which usually means that it has no sizing or glaze. It does not mean that the fabric has fixative on it. Even though the manufacturer has designated a type of fabric for dyeing or printing, this does not always mean that the fabric will take dye well; it may only mean that it has no sizing. If the fabric has been treated to resist wrinkles, it will resist dye also. These treatments cannot be removed without harmful chemicals. Test-dye unknown fabrics before purchasing large quantities.

## WEAVE

The type and quality of the weave influences dye results. A fine line will be difficult to paint on a heavily textured weave. A sateen weave will have more luster than a broadcloth. A very tight weave will have more fiber to accept the dye and result in darker colors than an open-weave fabric. Consider the use of the fabric after it is dyed; for example, some fabrics are hard to hand stitch, some will make better garments than others, and some are sturdier and better for outdoor use.

## WEIGHT

Thick fabric soaks up more dye than thin fabric and feels different to paint; you will need to apply more dye to thicker fabric to have dark colors. Printing on a thick fiber may only dye the top layer and not penetrate through. If the fabric is very thin or transparent, the colors will seem much lighter.

## COLOR

You can dye white fabric any color. If you start with colored fabric you limit the colors you can achieve. If the fabric is yellow, for example, you will not be able to dye it blue because dye is transparent and painting blue over yellow will make a green, depending on what intensity blue you use. If you dye over a very dark color, very little of your work will show. If you want white on the fabric, you have to leave places without dye, since there is no white dye.

## BASIC SUPPLIES

Gather the supplies listed on the next two pages: fabric, dye, auxiliary chemicals, measuring tools, containers and basic painting and printing tools. As you work, you will add to your supplies as needed and devise your own blocks, stamps, rollers and other tools for applying the colors to create a great variety of textures and patterns. Always keep your eyes open for tools in unexpected places.

Back, from left: Synthrapol SP, PRO Print Paste Mix SH, granular urea, 3 colors of powdered dye. Front, from left: soda ash, sodium alginate SH, Ludigol, long handled spoon, measuring spoons, dry measures, two dust/mist masks, liquid measure, rubber gloves.

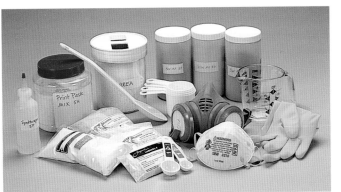

## SUPPLY LIST

The following is a list of supplies and the amounts you should
have on hand to do all 48 exercises in *Color by Design*. A few
more specialized supplies are listed in the individual chapters.

### FABRIC

| | |
|---|---|
| Mercerized cotton, broadcloth or print cloth | 22 yards (22 meters), any width |
| Silk, any medium to heavy weight | 2 yards (2 meters), any width |

### DYE POWDERS

| | | |
|---|---|---|
| Yellow MX-8G | 8 oz | (240 g) |
| Yellow MX-3RA | 4 oz | (120 g) |
| Red MX-8B | 8 oz | (240 g) |
| Red MX-5B | 4 oz | (120 g) |
| Blue MX-G | 8 oz | (240 g) |
| Turquoise MX-G | 4 oz | (120 g) |
| Black MX-CWNA | 4 oz | (120 g) |

### AUXILIARY CHEMICALS

| | | |
|---|---|---|
| Soda ash | 1 lb | (455 g) |
| Urea | 4 lbs | (3.5 k) |
| Sodium alginate SH | 1 lb | (455 g) |
| Metaphos | 1/2 lb | (225 g) |
| Synthrapol SP | 1 pint | (480 ml) |
| Optional: Ludigol | 1/2 lb | (225 g) |
| Optional: Pre-mixed print paste powder | 2 lb | (910 g) |

### FOR PREPARATION OF DYES AND AUXILIARIES

| | |
|---|---|
| Dust/mist mask | 1 |
| Rubber gloves | 2 pairs |
| Measuring spoons, plastic | 1 |
| Measuring cups for powders, plastic | 1 |
| 1-pint (480 ml) liquid measuring cup, plastic | 1 |
| Plastic spoons and forks | 10 |
| Long handled plastic spoon | 1 |
| Whisk | 1 |

### FOR STORAGE OF DYES AND CHEMICALS

| | |
|---|---|
| Plastic containers with tight lids to store powders | 6 |
| 16-oz (480 ml) plastic squeeze bottles and caps | 7 |
| 1-quart (960 ml) plastic containers for urea water, print paste | 2 |
| 1-gallon (3.8 liter) plastic container for soda solution | 1 |

### FOR MIXING COLORS

| | |
|---|---|
| White plastic palette, large | 1 |
| White plastic palette, small | 1 |
| Plastic containers to mix colors | 12 |

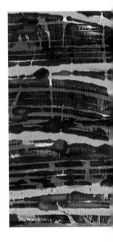

### PAINTING AND PRINTING TOOLS

| | |
|---|---|
| Bristle brushes, 1/2˝ - 3˝ (1.25 cm - 7.5 cm) | 3 |
| Nylon brushes, brights, rounds, and angled, sizes #0 - #12 | 6 |
| Sponge brushes, 1˝ (2.5 cm) | 4 |
| Sponge brushes, 2˝ (5 cm) | 2 |
| Sponge brushes, 4˝ (10 cm) | 2 |
| Textured sponges | 3 |
| Foam rollers, 1˝ - 12˝ (2.5 cm - 30 cm) | 4 |
| Plastic paint trays for rollers | 2 |
| Spray bottles, adjustable jet | 3 |
| Eye droppers | 3 |
| Needle-tip bottles | 2 |
| Soft lead pencil | 1 |
| Refillable felt pens | 3 |
| Masking tape rolls, various widths | 3 |

### GENERAL

| | |
|---|---|
| Rags and sponges for clean up | 6 |
| Light-weight plastic sheeting to cover fabric | 2 |
| Smooth washable white work surface, about 48˝ x 48˝ (120 cm x 120 cm) | 1 |

# INSTRUCTIONS

In this and subsequent chapters, measurements are given by volume (tsp, Tbs, cups, ml), which is sufficiently accurate and much easier than measuring by weight (oz, grams). More importantly, measuring by volume allows dyers to measure without lengthy exposure to dye powders. Although each color has a different density – for example, 1 tsp Red MX-8B weighs more than 1 tsp Turquoise MX-G – the amount of print paste used or the number of times a color is applied influences the results more than fractional differences in dye-powder weights.

Temperatures are given in each recipe to help define them; however, a thermometer is not necessary each time they are prepared.

## STEPS FOR SURFACE DYEING

Eight steps complete the process for surface application of Procion®MX dyes.

Thick colors spread on work surface and monoprinted on dry cotton, later low-water immersion dyed.

STEP 1  Prepare fabric by soaking in water with soda ash

STEP 2  Prepare print paste to thicken colors

STEP 3  Prepare urea water to thin print paste to desired consistency

STEP 4  Prepare dye concentrates

STEP 5  Mix dye concentrate, print paste, and/or urea water to desired consistency, color, and value

STEP 6  Apply dye mixture to soda-soaked fabric

STEP 7  Cure by letting dye bond with fibers

STEP 8  Wash out excess dye

## STEP 1   PREPARE FABRIC

Scour the fabric if it has sizing or other surface treatments. All silks should be scoured because they sometimes have streaks of silkworm gum in them which cannot be seen until the fabric is dyed. For more fabric information, see pages 20-23.

Scour the fabric by machine washing for 15 minutes as follows:

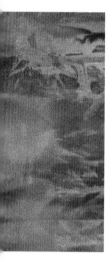

| | |
|---|---|
| Hot water | 140° F (60° C) |
| Soda ash | 1/2 tsp (2.5 ml) per 1 lb (455 g) fabric |
| Synthrapol SP | 1/2 tsp (2.5 ml) per 1 lb (455 g) fabric |

Prepare a soda solution and immerse the dry fabric for 5 to 20 minutes.

| | |
|---|---|
| Warm to hot water | 1 gallon (3.8 liters) |
| Soda ash | 9 Tbs (135 ml) |

The soda activates the fiber so it is ready to react with the dye when it is applied. Make sure the soda solution soaks thoroughly into the fabric; heavy fabrics will take longer. You can use the soda solution cold, but it may take longer to penetrate the fibers. If the fabric is only partly saturated, fewer fiber molecules will bond with the dye.

Once the fabric is soda-soaked, it can be dyed immediately, or it can be allowed to dry, either partially or entirely. I usually spin out the fabric in my washing machine, first making sure that no water will spray in during the spin cycle, which would dilute the soda ash concentration. I then let it line dry and fold it up to use whenever I need it. When using silk, I presoak it, let it dry, and store it in a very dry place, because the combination of soda and moisture can eventually damage silk fibers. Once the fabric is dry, it may be ironed on a medium setting.

## STEP 2    PREPARE PRINT PASTE

Print paste is the medium that carries the dye and controls its flow in the fibers. It contains urea, which maintains a minimum amount of moisture on the fabric during the time it is curing. The thickening agent is sodium alginate. Metaphos allows the alginate to flow more smoothly. Ludigol is an optional ingredient which can be helpful in achieving brighter Procion®MX colors in areas where the air is very polluted.

Mix the print paste, adding the ingredients in the following order.

| | |
|---|---|
| Warm to hot water | 3 cups (720 ml) |
| Granular urea | 6 1/2 Tbs (98 ml) |
| Metaphos | 1 1/2 tsp (7.5 ml) |
| Optional: Ludigol | 2 - 4 tsp (10 ml - 20 ml) |
| Sodium alginate SH | 6 tsp (30 ml) |
| Optional: extra sodium alginate | Up to 2 tsp (10 ml) more |
| Additional water | To total 1 quart (960 ml) |

Dissolve urea and metaphos in water, which cools as the urea dissolves. Add Ludigol, if needed. Gradually add the alginate and stir to minimize lumps. To make extra-thick print paste use a total of 8 tsp (40 ml) sodium alginate. Stir in additional water. Continue stirring at least 5 minutes. Allow to dissolve for 4 hours. If you have lots of lumps, let it sit overnight.

Instead of mixing the separate ingredients, I use a pre-measured dry mix available from several suppliers that contains the urea, sodium alginate SH, and metaphos. Measure the water according to package directions and add the mix while stirring. It is ready to use in about an hour. Make it thinner by adding urea water and thicker by adding more dry mix.

When I am working, I usually have print paste ready in several consistencies. My regular recipe of print paste mixed with an equal part dye concentrate makes thick colors. A medium print paste is good for many paint tools, especially rollers. A thin print paste is very watery and will make soft, blurry painted lines.

I occasionally mix extra-thick print paste for silk screen printing or monoprinting

### STEP 3   PREPARE UREA WATER

You will need urea water on hand when you want a print paste with a thinner consistency. Do not use tap water to thin print paste; it dilutes the urea concentration.

Stir until the urea dissolves.

| | |
|---|---|
| Warm to hot water | 1 cup (240 ml) |
| Granular urea | 7 tsp (35 ml) |

If you work in an extremely dry area, consider using 8 to 9 tsp (40 ml to 45 ml) urea. If you work in an extremely humid area, reduce to 6 tsp (30 ml).

### STEP 4   PREPARE DYE CONCENTRATES

This recipe produces dark colors when combined with an equal part of print paste or urea water. A little concentrate goes a long way, especially if you are dyeing pale colors. You may want to start by mixing half the recipe for each of the colors to see how far it goes.

Combine the ingredients in this order:

| | |
|---|---|
| Warm water | 1 cup (240 ml) |
| Granular urea | 2 - 4 Tbs (30 ml - 60 ml) |
| Dye powder | 2 Tbs (30 ml)<br>(double for black) |

Measure the warm water into a wide mouth container. *Do not* use water over 95° F (35° C) because this reduces the reactivity of the dye and will result in lighter colors. Add the granular urea and stir until almost dissolved. The water will cool. Put on your dust/mist mask and measure the dye powder into the urea water. Close the jar. Stir or shake the concentrate until all the dye is dissolved.

The urea in the dye concentrate recipe helps more dye-powder dissolve in less water than it would without urea. Each single-chemical color is a different chemical with a different weight and solubility, so some colors will dissolve with less urea than others. The recipe I use is based on an average weight of dye per table-spoon, so some of the dyes might not dissolve completely with smaller amounts of urea. Use more urea for the colors that you find do not dissolve in 2 Tbs (30 ml) urea. Once the concentrate is mixed, the value of the color you prepare with it can be adjusted by using different amounts of print paste and/or urea water.

Because Procion®MX dye will gradually bond with water at warmer temperatures, store the dye concentrate in a cool place. At room temperature, it will last about a week; refrigerated, it can last up to 20 weeks with reasonable strength. I have used dye concentrate months after making it without much visible loss of color. Make sure concentrates are at room temperature when ready to paint or print.

The strength of the dye concentrate can be tested by mixing it with an equal part print paste and painting it on soda-soaked fabric. Cure it, keep part of the piece unwashed, and wash the other part. When you compare them, you can see just how much wash-out has occurred. Under the correct conditions, the dry, unwashed sample should be very much like the dry, washed sample. If you have stored the dye concentrate too long, the washed sample will be a lot lighter.

### STEP 5   PREPARE COLORS

The recipe for dye concentrate is designed so that it can be mixed with the print paste (any consistency) and still dye a dark color.

Stir dye concentrate and print paste until smooth:

> Equal parts for a dark value
>
> Less dye concentrate for lighter colors

The color mixture has a honey-like consistency. Once blended, it does not separate. For a thinner mixture, add medium print paste, that is, regular print paste that is thinned with an equal part urea water. For pale values, add more print paste, either thinned with urea water or not, to the dye concentrate.

Remember, if the dye concentrate is below room temperature, it is cooler than required for reaction with the fibers. However, when mixed with print paste and urea water that have been stored at room temperature, it will be ready to use by the time you mix your secondary colors and make other preparations. It is best to prepare only enough thickened colors to use in one day. If you wish to store them, refrigerate. *Do not store colors if they have been contaminated with soda ash from painting tools that touched the soda on the fabric.*

### STEP 6   APPLY COLORS

This is the fun part. The color can be applied to soda-soaked fabric using any surface design technique. Use tiny brushes or giant ones, rollers, stamps, silk screen, sponges, wood blocks, squeegees, notched spreaders, squeeze bottles, spray bottles, or whatever tool makes the mark you like. The medium is extremely versatile. The colors can be applied thick or thin, to wet or dry fabric. (See Chapters 4 to 8.)

## STEP 7    CURE FABRIC

During curing, the soda ash used to soak the fabric in Step 1 creates a chemical bond between the dye and the fiber. You can cure the fabric when it is open or covered, flat or rolled. Each of these requirements has a wide range, and if conditions are within this range, your painted or printed fabrics will have very little color wash-out.

Three conditions are required to maximize the dye/fiber reaction:

| | |
|---|---|
| Time | 4 to 8 hours |
| Temperature | 70° F - 110° F (21° C - 43° C) |
| Moisture | Almost dry to the touch or very wet |

*Time:* Allow between 4 and 8 hours for the fabric to cure. The dye and fiber molecules need time to react. With surface applications, more time is required than when the fabric is immersed in a dye/water solution as in *Color by Accident,* because the ratio of water to dye is so much smaller. I usually let the fabric sit overnight before I let it dry completely. If I paint or print on the piece again, I wait another 4 to 8 hours for it to cure.

*Room temperature:* Work in the range of 70° F to 110° F (21° C to 43° C). If it is too cold, the reaction is slowed or stopped. When I know it will be colder in my studio, I use the space heater to maintain the temperature, particularly when I am working with turquoise or black or any very intense colors which might need more time and heat for curing.

*Moisture:* The molecules of dye can contact more dye sites on the fiber molecules when moisture is present, although the level of moisture required is so slight that the fabric can feel almost dry to the touch and still be sufficient for the reaction to occur. When the fabric becomes bone dry, the reaction will stop. Be aware that it is the indoor climate where you work that will determine the drying time; forced air heat, air conditioning, humidifiers, and dehumidifiers will affect how soon you should cover the fabric to maintain a small amount of moisture. When working with very little liquid (print paste/urea water/dye concentrate), such as when making fine lines, monitor the fabric's moisture while it is curing, and cover it when the fabric is almost dry so that colors will not smear. If the fabric is saturated with color, I may not cover it at all during the curing time. If you want the colors to bleed into each other and blend on the fabric, immediately covering the fabric will encourage that to happen.

### STEP 8   WASH OUT EXCESS DYE

The last and very necessary step in the dye process is to wash out all the chemicals and any unreacted dye. This need not be done immediately after curing, but must be done before the fabric is used. Once it has dried, you may want to dye it again before you wash out the excess dye and soda. Even unreacted Procion®MX dyes have a strong affinity for the fiber, so vigorous washing is necessary to remove them. Test the washed fabric while still wet by ironing it over dry white cotton. If color transfers, wash again.

Wash in warm water and Synthrapol, using these quantities. The final wash should be hot: 140° F (60° C).

| | |
|---|---|
| Hand wash | 1 tsp (5 ml) |
| Machine wash | 1 - 4 Tbs (15 ml - 60 ml) |

*Hot water*: Start with a warm rinse to get out some of the soda and dye. Then do one or more short washes with warm water and Synthrapol SP. The dye needs to be removed, not re-circulated with the fabric. If you move to hot water too quickly, the dye can transfer and stain other areas of the fabric. Silk is particularly susceptible to staining. The stronger the colors, the more care and the more washes you will need. Do not put the fabric in the dryer until it is completely washed because the moisture in the fabric and the heat of the dryer will cause any unreacted dye to bleed and stain. Check that the temperature of your hot water in your washing machine is 140° F (60° C).

*Agitation:* If the fabric is not agitated or stays tangled in hot water, the dye can transfer to places you didn't put it. Never leave it alone soaking in hot water without agitation and Synthrapol SP. I wash by machine as often as possible. I hand wash fabrics in special cases: fabric with a lot of black dye and white spaces, small pieces that may not open up in the washing machine, or silk that has taken me days to hand paint.

*Detergent:* Synthrapol SP is designed for soaping Procion® dyes. It does some of the work for dyers by scouring out unreacted dye. It also acts as a bit of insurance, helping keep dye particles in suspension and off the fibers while in the water. I use it in every step of the washing, then I rinse the fabric. Later, I wash the fabric as I would any other piece of laundry. If colors transfer in the wash, another hot water wash 140° F (60° C) with Synthrapol SP may fix the mistake.

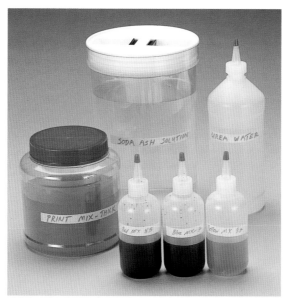

Mixed ingredients: print paste, soda solution, urea water and three colors of dye concentrate in squeeze bottles with yorker caps.

# SUMMARY OF DYEING RECIPES

### STEP 1 PREPARE FABRIC

If necessary, scour the fabric by machine washing for 15 minutes as follows:

| | |
|---|---|
| Hot water | 140° F (60° C) |
| Soda ash | 1/2 tsp (2.5 ml) per 1 lb (455 g) fabric |
| Synthrapol SP | 1/2 tsp (2.5 ml) per 1 lb (455 g) fabric |

Soak dry fabric in soda solution until it is thoroughly wet, 5 to 20 minutes.

| | |
|---|---|
| Warm to hot water | 1 gallon (3.8 liters) |
| Soda ash | 9 Tbs (135 ml) |

### STEP 2 PREPARE PRINT PASTE

Add ingredients in following order.

| | |
|---|---|
| Warm to hot water | 3 cups (720 ml) |
| Granular urea | 6 1/2 Tbs (98 ml) |
| Metaphos | 1 1/2 tsp (7.5 ml) |
| Optional: Ludigol | 2 - 4 tsp (10 ml - 20 ml) |
| Sodium alginate SH | 6 tsp (30 ml) |
| Optional: extra sodium alginate | Up to 2 tsp (10 ml) more |
| Additional water | To total 1 quart (960 ml) |

### STEP 3 PREPARE UREA WATER

Use to thin the print paste as needed.

| | |
|---|---|
| Warm to hot water | 1 cup (240 ml) |
| Granular urea | 7 tsp (35 ml) |

## STEP 4    PREPARE DYE CONCENTRATES

| | |
|---|---|
| Warm water | 1 cup (240 ml) |
| Granular urea | 2 - 4 Tbs (15 ml - 30 ml) |
| Dye powder | 2 Tbs (30 ml) (double for black) |

## STEP 5    PREPARE COLORS

Combine dye concentrate with print paste (any consistency).

Equal parts for a dark value

Less dye concentrate for lighter colors

## STEP 6    APPLY COLORS

Apply color (dye concentrate with print paste and/or urea water) to soda-soaked fabric. Use any surface design technique you choose (see Chapters 4 to 8).

## STEP 7    CURE FABRIC

Open or covered, flat or rolled.

| | |
|---|---|
| Time | 4 - 8 hours |
| Temperature | 70° F - 110° F (21° C - 43° C) |
| Moisture | Almost dry to the touch or very wet |

## STEP 8    WASH OUT EXCESS DYE

Wash in warm water and Synthrapol SP.
Final wash hot: 140° F (60° C).

| | |
|---|---|
| Hand wash | 1 tsp (5 ml) |
| Machine wash | 1 - 4 Tbs (15 ml - 60 ml) |

*Optional:* Test for wash fastness by ironing washed fabric while it is still wet over dry white cotton.

## TERMS USED FOR MIXTURES IN COLOR BY DESIGN

In the chapters and exercises that follow, these are the mixtures I intend for you to use when I refer to the terms below.

| | |
|---|---|
| Urea water | Regular recipe, with 7 tsp (35 ml) granular urea (page 36) |
| Print paste | Regular recipe, with 6 tsp (30 ml) sodium alginate SH (page 36) |
| Medium print paste | Print paste mixed with equal part urea water |
| Thin print paste | One part print paste and two parts urea water |
| Color | Dye concentrate mixed with print paste, any consistency |
| Thick color | Dye concentrate mixed with print paste |
| Medium-consistency color | Dye concentrate mixed with medium print paste |
| Medium-thin color | Dye concentrate mixed with thin print paste |
| Thin color | Dye concentrate mixed with only urea water |
| Double-strength color | Two parts dye concentrate with one part print paste and/or urea water |
| Extra-thick print paste | Prepared with 8 tsp (40 ml) sodium alginate SH |
| Extra-thick color | Dye concentrate mixed with extra-thick print paste |

# SHELF LIFE OF RECIPES

| ITEM | STORAGE | SHELF LIFE |
|------|---------|------------|
| Cotton soaked in soda | Dry | Indefinitely |
| Silk soaked in soda | Covered, dry | About a month |
| Dye powders | Sealed, dry, cool | 2 years, some much longer |
| All chemical powders | Sealed, dry, cool | Indefinitely |
| Soda solution | Covered, room temp | Indefinitely |
| Urea water | Covered, room temp | Until it smells of ammonia |
| Print paste | Covered, cool | Until it grows mold or smells of ammonia |
| Dye concentrate | Covered, room temp | 4 - 7 days |
| Dye concentrate | Covered, cool | 2 - 20 weeks |
| Colors (dye concentrate/ print paste) | Covered, cool | A day or two if no soda in it |
| Corn and potato dextrin, powder | Sealed, dry, cool | Indefinitely |
| Corn and potato dextrin, cooked | Sealed, cool | 1 - 15 days |

# COLOR MIXING

In this chapter, you will prepare colors and start painting. Each single-chemical color has slightly different characteristics of solubility, weight, reactivity, and temperature requirements, but generally they all work the same way and are good for mixing an unlimited array of colors. What you see on the fabric after you let the colors cure and dry is very close to the color you will have after it is washed and dried. When you put one color over another or if they flow together in the fabric when you paint, they mix in the fiber and you see a blended color. This transparency is a major factor in your decisions about placement of colors on your fabric. As you do the exercises, you will experience how they combine visually.

## S U P P L Y   L I S T / C H A P T E R   3

Have the following at hand before you begin the exercises.

| General: | White work surface, masking tape, palettes or cups, spoons and forks for mixing |
|---|---|
| Dye concentrate: | Yellow MX-8G, Red MX-8B, and Blue MX-G, 1/2 cup (120 ml) each |
| Auxiliaries: | Print paste, 2 cups (480 ml) and urea water, 1 cup (240 ml) |
| Fabric: | Dry, soda-soaked cotton: 4 fat quarters |
| Tools: | Several 1/2" - 1" (1.25 cm - 2.5 cm) brushes (any kind); optional: plastic measuring spoons |

Thickened colors painted with sponge brush on dry cotton. Where colors overlap, you see a new color.

## Paint a Color Wheel

Thickened Yellow MX-8G, Red MX-8B, Blue MX-G and their secondary colors painted in color wheel. Dark gray at center is mixed with unequal amounts of these.

*See supply list on page 41. For recipes, see pages 36 - 37.*

1. Prepare thickened primary colors – yellow, red, and blue – with each dye concentrate. Use about 2 Tbs (30 ml) print paste and same amount of dye concentrate in three separate cups or palette wells. Stir until each color is smooth.
2. With 1/2″ to 1″ (1.25 cm to 2.5 cm) brushes, dab each primary color in a triangle arrangement on fat quarter of dry, soda-soaked cotton.
3. Use thickened primary colors to make secondary colors – orange, green, and violet.
4. Dab each secondary color you mix along edge of fabric to see exactly what color it is.
5. Adjust secondary colors as needed by adding more yellow, red, or blue.
6. Paint them in place to create color wheel.

### OPTIONS

- Use Yellow MX-3RA, Red MX-5B, and Turquoise MX-G for color wheel.
- Mix and compare secondary colors made with different combinations of primary colors. For example, make orange by mixing Yellow MX-3RA and Red MX-8B, or by mixing Yellow MX-8G and Red MX-5B.
- Mix equal parts thickened yellow, red, and blue to see what color you get. Add small amounts of blue until it looks gray. Paint in middle of color wheel.

## Paint a Secondary Gradation

Blue to yellow
gradation painted
with thickened
colors on dry cotton.

*See supply list on page 41. For recipes, see pages 36 - 37.*

1. Prepare two thickened primary colors in separate cups as in previous exercise.
2. With 1″ (2.5 cm) brush, paint sample of one color on fat quarter of dry, soda-soaked cotton.
3. Add tiny bit of the other primary color to first color and stir well.
4. Paint new color on the fabric next to first.
5. Continue adding small amounts of second color to same cup, painting samples of each as you mix them. If you add a lot of second color, your gradation changes quickly; if you add less each time, it extends over more colors.
6. Mix and paint samples until you have color close to second primary you used.
7. Paint second primary as last color in gradation.

### OPTIONS
• Paint two more secondary gradations with other primary colors.
• Paint complement gradation. Start with primary color and add tiny bit of its complement – color opposite it on color wheel (page 42).
• Use Yellow MX-3RA, Red MX-5B, and Turquoise MX-G to paint three secondary gradations.

### TIP
When you clean
your brush, squeeze
dry. Excess water
dilutes chemicals
and makes colors run.

## Paint Blacks

Patches of thickened Yellow MX-8G, Red MX-8B, and Blue MX-G painted and partly over-lapped. First strip, left, shows mix of approximately equal amounts. Each strip shows results with addition of more colors as follows (left to right): blue, yellow, blue, blue, blue, red.

**T I P**

If you have a large amount of a color that will take a lot of a second color to change, take some out and then add small amounts of second color.

*See supply list on page 41. For recipes, see pages 36 - 37.*

1. Prepare double-strength primary colors in separate cups, using about 1 Tbs (15 ml) print paste and 2 Tbs (30 ml) dye concentrate. Black requires more dye concentrate to achieve darkest value possible.
2. With 1″ (2.5 cm) brushes, paint patches of each color on fat quarter of dry, soda-soaked cotton, overlapping to see how they combine.
3. Mix approximately equal parts of each of three thickened primary colors together in one cup.
4. Paint your mixture on fabric.
5. Add small amount of one primary color to mixture, stir, and paint on fabric. Keep adding colors and painting them until you have color that looks black to you.
6. After you get "black," keep adding small amounts of color and painting samples, so you can see subtle differences in blacks.
7. Keep about 1 Tbs (15 ml) of your best black for next exercise.

### OPTIONS

• Mix dark navy or deep burgundy red with double-strength primary colors.
• Rip off strip of fabric across painted stripes of blacks and reserve it unwashed to compare to your washed results.

## Paint a Value Gradation

Top: black from previous exercise. Medium-consistency print paste added gradually to make lighter values.

*See supply list on page 41. For recipes, see pages 36 - 37.*

1. Prepare medium print paste by combining equal parts of urea water and print paste, about 1/2 cup (120 ml) of each. Stir until smooth.
2. Using 1″ (2.5 cm) brush, paint a few strokes of your best black from previous exercise on fat quarter of dry, soda-soaked cotton.
3. Mix about 1 tsp (5 ml) of your black with about 1/2 tsp (2.5 ml) medium print paste.
4. Paint resulting value on fabric next to the first.
5. Continue adding about 1/2 tsp (2.5 ml) medium print paste and painting samples of each value until you have pale color. To avoid streaks of darker colors, clean brush after darkest values and stir each lighter value thoroughly before painting.

### OPTIONS

• Mix series of light tans from dark brown.
• Find piece of fabric or picture with a very light color you like and mix it.
• Paint a dark color. Wait for it to almost dry and paint over again. This may darken it, depending on how much dye was in first application.

# Practice the Applications

It is important to realize that the amount of control you have of how the colors flow depends on the amount of moisture you use in your applications. You can work on wet fabric with thin colors or on dry fabric with thick colors, or any variation in between. The colors can be applied with any tool that makes the mark you like. Painting with brushes or rollers, spraying, or using fine line tools will have various results, depending on how thick you prepare the colors and how much dye concentrate you use with them. You can also mask out portions of the fabric or manipulate it with pleats or wrinkles before you work. Printing techniques are equally numerous. You might use sponges, stamps, silk screens, or blocks. Or you may do rubbings, direct monoprinting, or any combination of these.

Water-soluble resists are an exciting way to increase design possibilities with surface applications of thickened dye on fabric. There are some prepared resists that work well and two resists which require cooking that are very successful: corn dextrin and potato dextrin.

Using successive layers of surface applications of color works well with Procion®MX dye. It is quickly apparent that the more layers you use, the less predictable – and more interesting – the results.

Explore and learn and have fun. Do some of the exercises more than once, try as many of the options as you can, stay on the look-out for new tools, and have an open mind about how your final piece of fabric should appear.

Large piece of silk using many different applications, including: roller impressions, rubbings, sponge brush, line work, water-soluble resist, masking, and sponge prints.

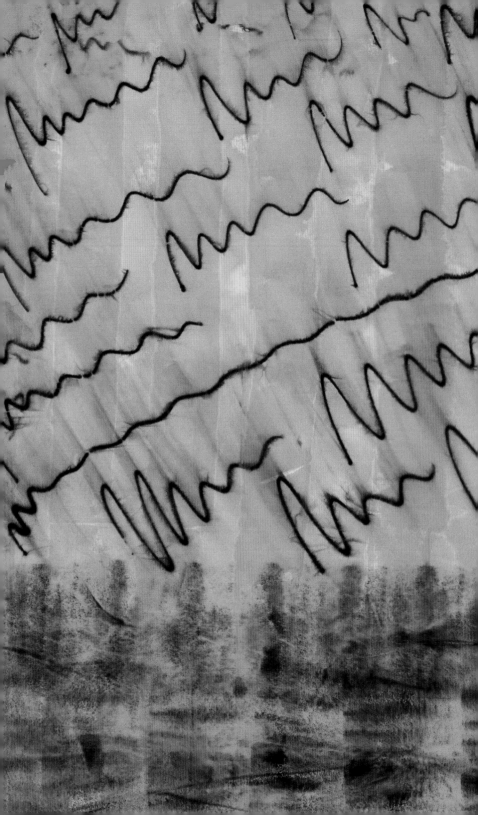

# MOISTURE VARIATIONS

If you vary the amount of moisture when you apply the colors, a variety of results are possible. Logic applies here: if you are in a humid place or work on wet fabric and apply a lot of dye, it may spread more than it would if you were in a dryer place, or if you used dry fabric and scant amounts of dye. The larger the area covered by the same amount of dye, the lighter in value the resulting color appears. You can create a very soft-edged line or a crisp, hard edge. You can make the dye flow in spidery lines across the fabric or separate into a halo of another color around the shape you paint. If you paint or print colors over wet print paste, you can move the dye around a bit and blend the colors, resulting in blurred edges or soft gradations. The exercises in this chapter will allow you to experience some of these possibilities.

Another important variable in controlling the flow of the colors is the amount of moisture present when the fabric is left to cure. You should always *monitor the moisture* of your fabric as it cures. You must maintain a minimum of moisture in the fabric for 4 to 8 hours to maximize the reaction between the dye and fiber. In a humid place, the fabric may not dry during the whole length of the curing time, in which case it does not need to be covered. However, if you want to encourage the spreading of the colors, you should cover it with plastic. If you want a hard, crisp edge, control the thickness of the dye and the amount applied, encourage most of the moisture to evaporate, and cover the fabric before it gets completely dry. Always cover the fabric if it becomes almost dry to the touch before 4 hours have passed.

Bands of thin yellows were applied on dry fabric with a wide sponge brush. While the fabric was still wet, thick black was applied with a roller and needle-tip bottle.

## SUPPLY LIST / CHAPTER 4

Have the following at hand before you begin the exercises.

| | |
|---|---|
| General: | White work surface, masking tape, palettes or cups, spoons and forks for mixing, paper towels, plastic sheeting |
| Dye concentrate: | Yellow MX-8G, Red MX-8B, and Blue MX-G, 1/2 cup (120 ml) each |
| Auxiliaries: | Soda solution, print paste, urea water, 2 cups (480 ml) each |
| | Synthrapol SP, 1/2 cup (120 ml) |
| Fabric: | Dry, soda-soaked cotton: 3 fat quarters |
| | Cotton without soda: 3 fat quarters and one 1/2 yard (meter) piece |
| Tools: | Select various sizes/shapes from Painting and Printing Tools on page 25. |

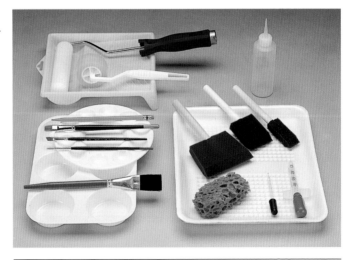

Tools used for fabrics in Chapter 4. Clockwise from top left: sponge rollers in paint tray, needle-tip bottle, sponge brushes, textured sponge and eye droppers on disposable tray, bristle brush on large palette, #2 pencil, small nylon brushes on a small palette.

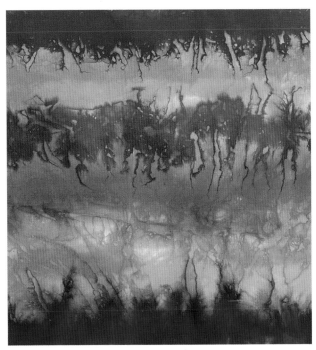

# Thin on Wet: Primary

Wet, soda-soaked fabric, painted with thin colors using sponge brush. After about 15 minutes, fabric was covered with plastic and pressed.

*See supply list on page 50. For recipes, see pages 36 - 37.*

1. Dip one fat quarter cotton (without soda) in soda solution and wring out.
2. Put wet fabric on plastic sheeting on work surface.
3. Prepare thin primary colors in three separate cups – about 1 Tbs (15 ml) dye concentrate and an equal amount urea water.
4. Apply two or three thin colors on fabric with brush or eye dropper. Leave 1˝ to 2˝ (2.5 cm to 5 cm) between colors to allow for spreading.
5. Create lighter values by adding 1 tsp to 2 tsp (5 ml to 10 ml) urea water to each thin color and apply to fabric.
6. Dilute lighter values again with urea water and apply to fabric.
7. After 5 to 15 minutes, cover with plastic and press, spreading colors. Leave wrapped until cured.

## OPTIONS
• Repeat exercise, but leave fabric undisturbed after last color is applied and uncovered to cure.
• Compare flow of dye with two pieces, one slightly damp, one saturated with soda solution.
• Use different primary colors and see if they flow differently or make different colored halos.

**TIP**
The wetness of the fabric not only spreads the colors, but also dilutes them. Using more than half dye concentrate with the urea water may result in darker colors.

51

## Thin on Wet: Secondary

Wet fabric wrinkled on work surface and painted with thin dark colors.

*See supply list on page 50. For recipes, see pages 36 - 37.*

1. Dip fat quarter of cotton (without soda) in soda solution and wring out.
2. Place wet fabric on work surface, wrinkling it until it is about half original size.
3. Prepare thin primary color with each dye concentrate, as in previous exercise, in three separate cups. Use these to mix secondary colors, orange, green, and violet in three separate cups.
4. Apply secondary colors in widely spaced places with brush or eye dropper.
5. Mix a neutral by combining small amounts of the thin secondary colors.
6. Drop or paint it on the fabric between other colors.
7. Cover fabric with plastic while it cures.

### OPTIONS

- Prepare secondary colors with double-strength thin primary colors and apply to wet fabric.
- Place small objects (like rubber washers or split peas) under wet fabric before applying colors. Leave undisturbed until cured.
- Dunk and wring a skein of cotton, rayon, or silk yarn in soda solution. Paint on thin colors.

Rayon/cotton knit yarn, soaked in soda solution and painted with thin colors.

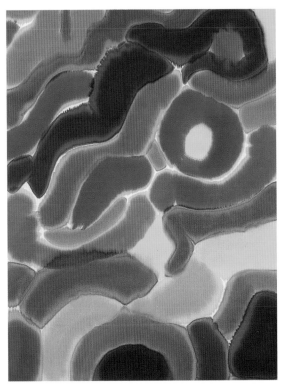

## Thin on Dry

Thin colors painted on dry, soda-soaked cotton. The colors flow and separate into the white space left around them.

*See supply list on page 50. For recipes, see pages 36 - 37.*

1. Prepare thin primary color with each dye concentrate, about 2 Tbs to 3 Tbs (30 ml to 45 ml) of each.
2. Mix thin secondary colors with thin primary colors, using six separate cups altogether, as in previous exercise.
3. Apply colors to fat quarter dry, soda-soaked cotton with sponge brush, leaving at least 2″ (5 cm) between each color. When given space to flow, mixed colors separate. The single-chemical colors flow at different rates, according to their weight and reactivity, producing a halo effect around brush mark.
4. Cover with plastic during cure time.

### OPTIONS

• Do the same exercise on dry, soda-soaked silk.
• Paint thin colors on dry, soda-soaked cotton without leaving any space between colors.
• Mix thin blacks using different red, yellow, and blue MX dyes. Paint them on dry, soda-soaked cotton.

**TIP**

Painting thin color on fabric is a good test to see if it is a single-chemical color or a mixed color. A halo will appear around a mixed color if allowed to spread.

# Thick on Wet

Wet, soda-soaked fabric, painted with thick black dye on sponge brush and with needle-tip bottle. Color spreads and blurs into white ground because fabric is wet, but much less than it would if thin colors were used.

**T I P**
You can dip dry, soda-soaked fabric in soda solution and use it wet if you wish.

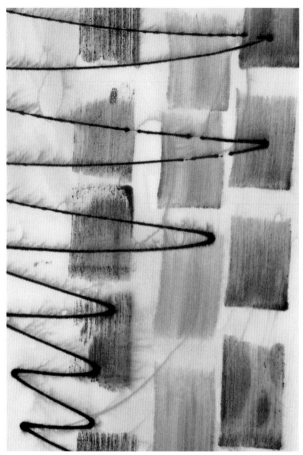

*See supply list on page 50. For recipes, see pages 36 - 37.*

1. Dip fat quarter cotton (without soda) in soda solution and wring out.
2. Stretch wet fabric flat on work surface.
3. Mix thick colors with each primary, about 1 Tbs (15 ml) dye concentrate and equal amount of print paste in three separate cups.
4. Use thick primary colors to make secondary colors or black.
5. Paint using at least two different tools. The wetter the fabric and the more you apply in one place, the more the color will spread.

OPTIONS
• Paint thick primary colors across and over each other on wet fabric.
• Mix and paint a thick brown on wet fabric. Add urea water and paint again. Repeat until it is very thin.

# Thick on Dry

Outlines of these
shapes were marked
with pencil and
colors were painted
in with nylon brushes
and thickened colors
on dry, soda-soaked
fabric.

*See supply list on page 50. For recipes, see pages 36 - 37.*

1. Stretch and tape down corners of fat quarter of dry, soda-soaked cotton.
2. Prepare thick primary colors with each dye concentrate.
3. Mix colors you wish to use from these.
4. Prepare several lighter values in more cups by adding medium-consistency print paste to some colors.
5. Mark lines on fabric with soft lead pencil. If pencil is not too dark, lines will wash out with excess dye.
6. Paint evenly using your lines as guides. Change to a small pointed (round or angled) brush to paint dye in points or small spaces. If you place too much dye close to line, it may flow across, so brush it away or use a paper towel to blot it.
7. Monitor moisture during curing. Let fabric get almost dry to touch, then cover it lightly with plastic.

## OPTIONS

• When colors feel dry, paint more over them.
• While colors are still wet, blend darker colors over them.

**T I P**
Pale colors are
harder to paint
evenly without
strokes showing
than dark colors.

## Paint Over Thick

Dry, soda-soaked cotton, painted with clear print paste, then thickened colors blended over top using smooth sponge brush.

*See supply list on page 50. For recipes, see pages 36 - 37.*

### TIP

Using print paste as first layer dilutes value of colors applied on top. You can compensate for this by using more dye concentrate in colors.

1. Stretch and tape fat quarter dry, soda-soaked cotton firmly onto work surface.
2. Paint medium print paste evenly all over fabric with wide sponge brush.
3. While it is still wet, paint on medium or dark value of thick color, smoothing out brush strokes. Working on top of print paste allows you more time to spread colors around than is possible with dry fabric.
4. Blot with paper towel if it is very moist.
5. Blend second thick color over part of first color with smooth brush. Rubbing with paper towel soon after dye is applied can help smooth colors. More colors can be worked in as you wish.

### OPTIONS

- Blend complementary colors on base of wet print paste.
- Paint shapes with pale thick colors. While wet (blot if very wet) add shading with dark colors.
- Draw an object you can look at as you paint, such as apple, pear, or head of garlic. Paint with thick colors, then add shadows. If object is complicated, draw on paper first, then trace it onto fabric.

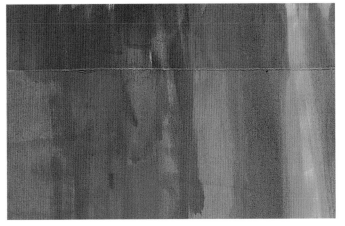

## Test Your Results

A test strip torn from fabric and saved unwashed. The larger piece is washed and dried. It almost matches the dry test strip.

*See supply list on page 50. For recipes, see pages 36 - 37.*

1. Tear off 2″ (5 cm) strip from one side of each of several pieces of fabric that have been cured but not yet washed.
2. Wash larger part of fabric (page 34), using 1 tsp (5 ml) Synthrapol SP or more depending on amount of fabric to wash. Leave test strips unwashed.
3. Dry fabrics and compare each to dry test strip. Colors and values of larger pieces should be very much the same as test strips. If they are much lighter, check list of possible reasons (page 147).

### OPTIONS
• Compare washed and unwashed results of piece that was painted while wet with those from piece that was painted while dry.
• Test piece that was painted with clear print paste first (see Paint Over Thick on page 56).
• Test some of fabric you paint and print throughout your first year of playing with Procion® MX dyes.

You can see relative value of colors as you paint (upper), but actual value cannot be judged until fabric is dry (middle). After fabric is washed (lower), it should look the same as it looked when it was dry but still unwashed.

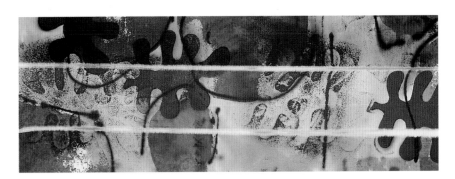

## Combine Wet and Dry

Controlling the amount of moisture is the key to creating many different effects with surface applications of dye. When you wish to work with wet and dry effects on the same piece of fabric, pay attention to the moisture content of the fabric and the consistency of the colors before you apply the dye.

Combination of thick and thin colors painted on dry, soda-soaked fabric. Thickness of colors and amount of space between them determines how much they spread and flow together.

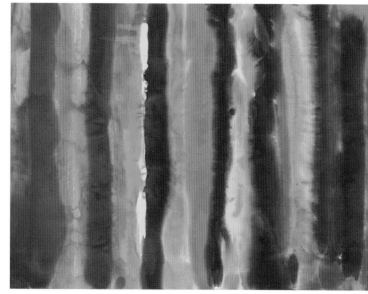

Pale colors were brushed onto dry, soda-soaked cotton, then thick black dye was applied with pointed bottle.

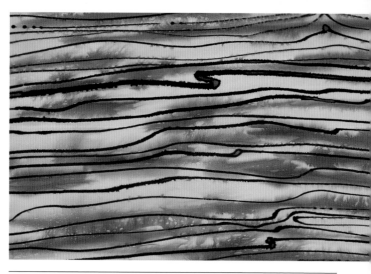

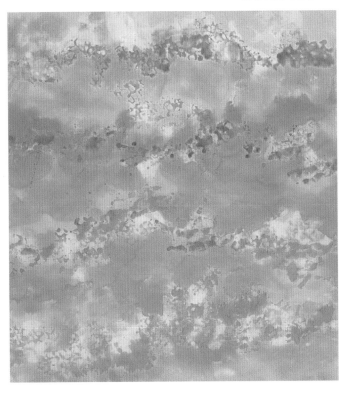

## Combine Wet and Dry
*continued*

*See supply list on page 50. For recipes, see pages 36 - 37.*

1. Use a bristle brush or textured sponge to apply print paste (without dye concentrate) in several places on a 1/2 yard (meter) dry, soda-soaked cotton.
2. Do the same with several thick colors, leaving spaces between marks.
3. Prepare several values of thin colors and apply them around on the fabric. Allow them to spread.
4. Continue to paint more colors, either thick or thin. Avoid creating puddles that may result in colors that wash out. If fabric gets too wet, blot with paper towel and paint more or leave it to cure.

### OPTIONS

• On dry piece of fabric, paint several areas of light value, thick colors. Paint thin colors near thick colors and see how they blend.
• Paint thin colors with wide brush all over a dry piece of fabric, then, before it is dry, apply thickened colors with sponge or brush.
• Paint thin lines on dry fabric, allow to sit for 5 to 15 minutes, then cover with pale color.

Clear print paste and thickened colors applied with a textured sponge on dry, soda-soaked fabric. Thin colors were applied around thick colors and then more thick color was painted in a few places.

# PAINT TECHNIQUES

One reason to vary the viscosity of the colors is that thick and thin colors flow on the fabric differently when you paint them. Another reason is to make them work well with the tools you select. A wide bristle brush will not give a dry-brush mark if the dye is mixed too thin. A soft brush with a point will not make a smooth line if the dye is too thick. Rollers can make a solid mark, a speckled effect, parallel lines, and repeat patterns. They can "remember" an impression and take a rubbing, depending on how you handle them and the consistency of the colors. Thick colors can be masked out very simply with paper, tape, and other shapes placed on the fabric. If the color is mixed too thin, it flows right under the mask. The fabric itself can be manipulated before it is painted or sprayed, creating shapes with the folds of the fabric. Again, the tool you choose and the consistency of the colors are key to your results.

Thick colors applied with rollers and brushes, some painted directly on dry fabric, others blended over another color. Red dye concentrate in felt tip pen painted over dried area of thick-ened yellow dye.

## S U P P L Y   L I S T / C H A P T E R   5

Make sure you have the following at hand before you begin the exercises in this chapter.

| | |
|---|---|
| General: | White work surface, masking tape, palettes or cups, spoons and forks for mixing, paper towels, plastic sheeting. For spraying: dust/mist mask. |
| Dye concentrate: | Yellow MX-8G, Red MX-8B, Blue MX-G, and Black MX-CWNA, 1/2 - 1 cup (120 - 240 ml) each |
| Auxiliaries: | Soda solution, print paste, urea water, 2- 3 cups (480 - 720 ml) each |
| Fabric: | Dry, soda-soaked cotton: 1 fat quarter and eight 1/2 yard (meter) pieces |
| | Cotton without soda: 1/2 yard (meter) piece |
| | Dry, soda-soaked silk: 1 fat quarter |
| Tools: | Select various sizes/shapes from Painting and Printing Tools on page 25 and from the following: rubber washers, tile separators or other low-relief firm objects that will make an impression on a roller. |

Additional tools used in Chapter 5, from left: shaped and textured rollers, spray bottle, foam roller in paint trays, leaves, masking tape, rubber washers, tile separators, sponge blocks, wood block, specialty rollers, fuzzy sponge tool, air pen, refillable felt pens, wide bristle brush, notched sponge brushes.

## Large Brushes

Upper: samples
of strokes and lines
made with 1″
(2.5 cm) nylon
bristle brush.
Lower: different
strokes with 3″
(7.5 cm) sponge
brush and thick black.

*See supply list on page 62. For recipes, see pages 36 - 37.*

1. Prepare about 1/2 cup (120 ml) of one thick color, using equal parts dye concentrate and print paste.
2. Using different strokes and angles with a brush (sponge, bristle, or nylon of any size), paint as many kinds of marks as you can on 1/2 yard (meter) dry, soda-soaked cotton. Use brush as a stamp, as well as stroking with it.
3. Choose another brush or brushes and make similar marks. You will find that thick colors work better with some brushes than with others.

### OPTIONS

• Prepare same color with half dye concentrate and half medium print paste. Paint on dry fabric. Compare results.
• Prepare same color with half dye concentrate and half urea water. Paint with same tools.
• Do same exercise on wet, soda-soaked fabric.

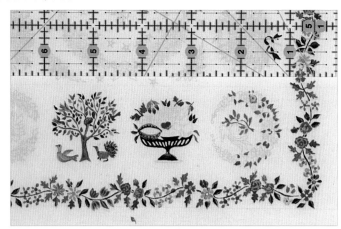

## Small Brushes

Dry, soda-soaked silk stretched over pattern and painted with #000 round nylon brush. For this kind of detail combine dye with medium or thin print paste. Fabric is not yet washed.

**TIP**

Have a paper towel handy while you paint to blot any color that starts to spread.

 *See supply list on page 62. For recipes, see pages 36 - 37.*

1. Iron fat quarter of dry, soda-soaked silk with medium heat and stretch it on smooth, hard surface about same size as fabric, so it can be turned easily for painting.
2. Prepare 1/4 cup (60 ml) each of medium print paste and thin print paste.
3. Prepare about 2 Tbs (30 ml) of each primary color by mixing equal parts dye concentrate and medium print paste. Mix secondary colors from these.
4. Mix about 2 Tbs (30 ml) of each primary color by mixing equal parts dye concentrate and thin print paste. Mix secondary colors from these.
5. Using several small nylon brushes, practice making shapes and lines with colors of various consistencies.
6. Choose several colors, medium or medium-thin consistency, and make lighter values by mixing in small amounts of thin print paste.
7. Fill fabric. You will find that you can judge how much dye a brush will carry and how much pressure to use when painting to create the shape or line you want. Small brushes, needed for small marks, don't hold much dye and may need several applications.
8. Cover fabric as soon as it feels dry to touch.

### OPTIONS

- Draw detailed design in pencil on soaked, ironed fabric. Paint in shapes with small brushes.
- Try shading shapes you painted with more colors before first colors dry.
- Stretch silk over a plastic transparency of a tiny design. Black lines show through most white fabrics. Paint using tiny brushes, size #0 to #000. Cover whenever you stop working.

# Rollers

By alternately pressing and lifting a smooth, 4″ (10 cm) sponge roller in vertical and horizontal lines, a weave-like effect is created. Background colors were sprayed on wrinkled, dry fabric.

*See supply list on page 62. For recipes, see pages 36 - 37.*

1. Tape down corners of 1/2 yard (meter) dry, soda soaked cotton.
2. Prepare one or more colors by mixing dye concentrates and medium print paste, because thinner colors work better with rollers.
3. Practice making different marks with rollers by varying your pressure on the handle, by changing the direction of the stroke, or by pressing harder on one side of roller as you apply colors.
4. Fill whole piece of fabric.
5. After it is partially dry, paint or roll on colors in background.

## OPTIONS

- Try different textured roller. The type of fiber or sponge used will change the kind of line you get.
- Find a selection of sizes and types of rollers that will make different kinds of lines.
- Paint plaid using different widths of rollers, overlapping colors to get mixed colors. Fill in background with light color.

**T I P**
Foam rollers clean up more easily than fiber rollers.

## Adapted Rollers

Fabric was painted with thin, pale blues. While it was still wet, two 4″ (10 cm) rollers were used to make dots and wavy lines. One roller has felt dots glued to it; the other is cut into four rounds so that it makes four parallel lines.

*See supply list on page 62. For recipes, see pages 36 - 37.*

1. Tape down corners of 1/2 yard (meter) dry, soda-soaked cotton.
2. Prepare several colors using medium print paste.
3. Adapt one or more rollers by cutting in notches or lines or by adding felt shapes, string, or other materials.
4. Practice using your rollers on half the piece of fabric. How evenly color is applied on the roller and how you press when you roll will determine the kind of marks you make.
5. Lightly dampen other half of fabric with soda solution on a sponge.
6. Use your rollers on wet fabric to see what kind of patterns they make. Experiment by varying pressure on roller.

### OPTIONS

- Put more than one color in paint tray without mixing and see what color combinations appear when you roll.
- Find sponge roller without hard center. If you cut the roller into pieces at angles, it will make lines that get wide, then narrow.
- Pick texture you want to use such as grass, granite, or bark and design a few rollers that create your desired effect.

# Roller Impressions

Circular rubber washers and x-shaped tile spacers were used to make impressions on dense sponge roller with thickened black.

*See supply list on page 62. For recipes, see pages 36 - 37.*

1. Tape down corners of 1/2 yard (meter) dry, soda-soaked cotton.
2. Prepare one or more colors with dye concentrate and medium print paste.
3. Select a variety of hard, firm shapes, such as rubber washers or tile separators. Place them on work surface, next to fabric.
4. Fill roller evenly with color. Roll once, firmly, over shapes. The foam roller will hold impression of shapes for a short time.
5. Immediately roll onto fabric. Use even pressure appropriate to amount and thickness of color in roller. Pressing too hard with a saturated roller results in blurs. Pressing too lightly results in very faint impressions. Notice that the impression has to be refreshed. When you re-do the impression, you may get multiples in one roll.

## OPTIONS

- Cut your own shapes from linoleum, hard rubber, or Styrofoam to make your roller impressions.
- See how negative shapes made by roller impressions appear to pop out when you brush on a light color later.
- Make both positive and negative impressions with same shapes. Put a shape under fabric and roll over it. The roller will hold the impression when you roll again on the fabric without the shape under it.

## TIP

Some sponge rollers are too soft to hold an impression.

## Mask Out

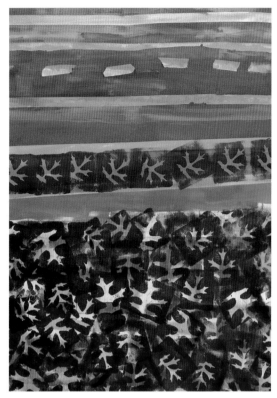

Thick colors were brushed on dry fabric over strips of masking tape. Thin colors were painted in white areas after tape was lifted. Below, colors were rolled on in overlapping lines. Then, leaves were placed over dry colors and another layer of dark color was applied.

*See supply list on page 62. For recipes, see pages 36 - 37.*

1. Tape down corners of 1/2 yard (meter) dry, soda-soaked cotton.
2. Prepare several colors with print paste or medium print paste.
3. Rip or cut wide masking tape and place it on fabric in a pattern, rubbing edges down.
4. Brush or roll colors over tape. Tape can be removed while fabric is still wet, if you wish. If dye is too thin or pushed under tape, you may not have a sharp edge when you pull it away.
5. Fill in white spaces, if you wish, with any consistency colors.

OPTIONS
- Apply tape and a light color. Wait for fabric to get dry to the touch, then move tape and apply a darker color.
- Find shapes in nature or in your home to use as masks. It is more difficult to get sharp edges with objects that don't stick to fabric.
- Make stencil from thin, stiff plastic. If stencil is very detailed, consistency of dye and pressure on roller or brush are even more important.

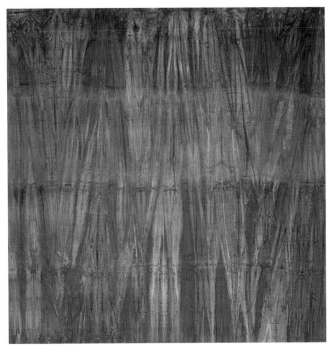

## Manipulated Fabric, Wet

Thick blue and yellow were applied with brushes to wet, pleated, and folded soda-soaked cotton.

*See supply list on page 62. For recipes, see pages 36 - 37.*

1. Prepare 1/2 cup (120 ml) each of two or three medium-thin colors. (Use equal parts thin print paste and dye concentrate.)
2. Dunk 1/2 yard (meter) cotton without soda into soda solution. Wring out excess and fold or wrinkle the fabric any way you wish on work surface.
3. Roll one color on one side of folds.
4. Turn fabric over without disturbing folds too much.
5. Roll second color on other side of folds. Check inside folds to see how much white is left. Make adjustments in folds if you wish and paint in more of one of the colors or a third color. Every fold you make will create a mark on fabric. Be aware of many possibilities, including diagonal and radiating pleats.
6. Spread flat or leave it folded to cure. Each will give a different result.

### OPTIONS

• Do same folding or wrinkling, but use thin colors.
• Sew texture, using smocking, pleating or other stitching techniques. Then wet fabric in soda solution and apply medium-thin or thin colors.
• Wrap wet, soda-soaked fabric on pole, push it together to make wrinkles, then paint with thin colors.

**TIP**
Thick colors do not penetrate through the fabric as much as thin colors do.

## Manipulated Fabric, Dry

Roller was dipped in thick red and blue and rolled over wood block. The impression was applied to wrinkled, dry cotton. Later, fabric was low-water immersion dyed.

*See supply list on page 62. For recipes, see pages 36 - 37.*

1. Arrange 1/2 yard (meter) dry, soda-soaked cotton with wrinkles or folds on work surface.
2. Prepare one or more medium or thick colors.
3. Roll short strokes over some wrinkles. If you press lightly you will not see edges of roller. If you press firmly, roller may "remember" the impression of wrinkles.
4. Flatten fabric and wrinkle again, rolling colors over wrinkles.
5. Repeat until fabric has lots of visual texture.
6. Paint background, either while it is still wet or after it gets dry to touch. Use any consistency colors.

### OPTIONS

• Create set of secondary patterns as you roll by putting impressions on roller each time before you put it on wrinkled fabric.
• Make a directional design by wrinkling fabric widthwise, lengthwise, or diagonally.
• Use tape or stitches to hold wrinkles in fabric before you roll on colors.

# Spray

Upper: dry cotton was wrinkled, then sprayed with thin black from one direction and then with several thin colors from other side.

Lower: dry fabric was twisted to make wrinkles, then sprayed with thin black, red, and yellow.

*See supply list on page 62. For recipes, see pages 36 - 37.*

1. Place 1/2 yard (meter) dry, soda-soaked cotton on plastic *outdoors,* but out of the wind. Manipulate fabric with folds or leave it flat.
2. Prepare one or more thin colors. (Equal parts dye concentrate and urea water will make darker colors; less dye concentrate will make lighter colors.) Fill spray bottles, one for each color.
3. *Put on dust/mist mask.*
4. Test spray pattern on a piece of newspaper and adjust spray the way you want it.
5. Spray fabric a few times. If you hold the sprayer at an angle to fabric, wrinkles will stop dye and other side of wrinkle will not get sprayed.
6. Rearrange fabric and spray again. First few sprays make speckles on dry fabric, but when sprayed over a wet color a soft blend results. Avoid spraying so much that dye puddles, which will wash out soda needed to fix colors.

## OPTIONS

• Let fabric get almost dry between spraying different colors. This will produce more speckles and spots.
• Spray dye on soda-soaked t-shirts. Color will spread differently in a knit.
• Place shapes on fabric with masking tape. Combine 2 cups (480 ml) thin color with 1 Tbs (15 ml) print paste, so color will flow slightly less when it hits fabric.

# Fine Line Tools

Upper half: clear print paste was painted and allowed to dry, then lines were drawn with felt tip pens filled with straight dye concentrate. Lines on lower half were drawn directly on dry soda-soaked fabric with air pen and different sized points using thick colors.

*See supply list on page 62. For recipes, see pages 36 - 37.*

1. Tape down corners of dry, soda-soaked fat quarter of cotton.
2. Select two or more fine line tools. Prepare colors that have consistency that works best with tool selected. Quality of line is determined by type of tool used, thickness of dye, and speed and pressure of application. If using needle-tip bottle, use thick color. Rest tip on fabric and pull. If using felt pens, thickened dye will not flow through felt. Use full-strength dye concentrate and paint over dry print paste for dark, hard-edged line. If using air pen, best consistency of color to use is determined by point you choose. If using fine brush, medium-thin colors work best.
3. Draw lines; practice making the kinds of lines you like all over the fabric.

## OPTIONS

- After painting lines, wait two minutes, then paint in thin colors over half the fabric. Wait two hours, then do the same to other half.
- Do line drawing over still-wet background color. Compare results to above exercise.
- Draw a series of shapes, wait until they are almost dry to touch, then fill in with thick colors.

Many, many kinds of marks can be made with a few simple tools. Brushes, rollers, sprayers, and masking tape can create even more variations. The way the line or mark finally appears on the fabric is determined by the viscosity of the colors, the wetness of the fabric, and the hand of the dyer. Dyes are transparent colors and can be layered on top of each other, with the earlier applications showing through the later ones.

## Combine Paint Techniques

Thick gray was applied on dry, soda-soaked silk with pre-cut sponge roller. Sponge brushes were used to paint all other marks. Light gray shows through red because it was applied first.

## Combine Paint Techniques

*continued*

*See supply list on page 62. For recipes, see pages 36 - 37.*

A roller cut at angles was used with thickened orange to make wide and narrow lines. A solid roller made wide marks with a dotted texture and impressions of a spiral block. Dark lines were drawn on wet.

1. Prepare colors for use with line tools.
2. Draw lines on 1/2 yard (meter) dry, soda-soaked cotton.
3. Use roller with thickened color to fill in some of background. Use variety of types of line and roller marks described in this chapter. Remember that consistency of colors and pressure on the roller determine whether you get a solid line or speckles.
4. Add more lines while fabric is still wet, or wait until color is dry to touch before you add them.
5. Fill in background using thin dye on sponge brush, either immediately or after about an hour.

### OPTIONS

• Create a pattern by alternating brush marks and roller marks and by alternating light and dark values.
• Spray or paint shapes on fabric, then use line tool to emphasize edges of shapes. Paint thin colors in background areas.
• Create all-over design on wrinkled fabric, using adapted rollers. Flatten fabric and add details with small brush or line tool.

## Combine Paint Techniques
*continued*

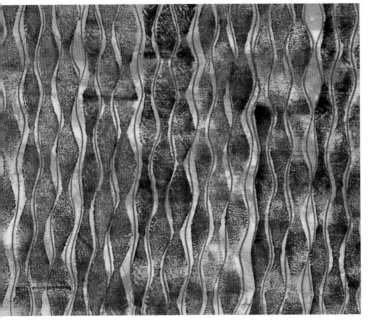

Both pieces of fabric use same roller with angle cuts. Upper piece was done on dry fabric and thickened red and yellow were painted in around roller lines. Lower piece was painted with thin colors and while it was wet, roller marks and narrow lines were made with thick colors.

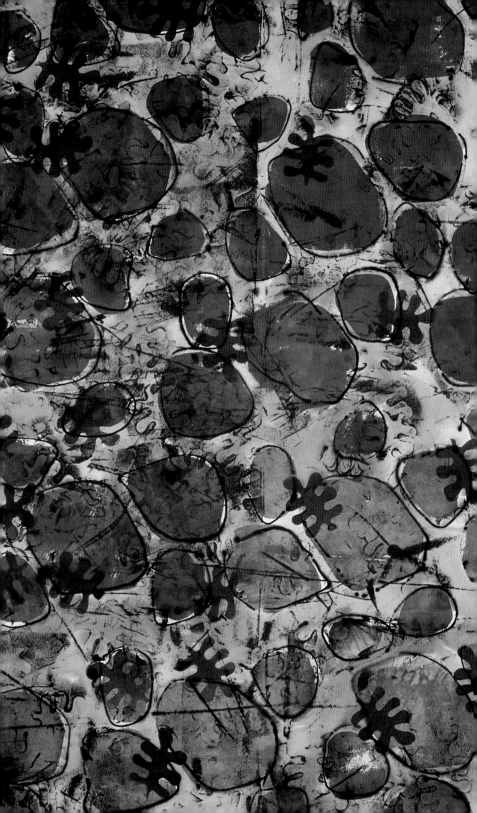

# PRINT TECHNIQUES

Repeat designs can be made with brushes and rollers, but they are even more easily made with blocks and sponges and other printing tools. The same principles hold true with printing as with painting: the consistency of the colors, the wetness of the fabric, and the hand of the dyer will determine how the printed marks finally look on the fabric. Remember, colors overlapped on each other become combinations; the first color on the fabric, however light, influences later colors.

Thickened Procion®MX dyes are very effective for use with blocks, rubbings, monoprints, and silk screens. You can make exact repetitions of identical designs, or designs and patterns with unlimited variations that flow and change according to how the dye is applied and the colors mixed.

Self-adhesive shelf paper with stone shapes was applied to pre-stretched silk screen. Several thick colors were pulled at same time with squeegee. Later, pale thin colors were painted in background and thick black was used for lines and leaf stamp. Impressions on the roller made negative leaf shapes.

## S U P P L Y    L I S T / C H A P T E R    6

Have the following at hand before you begin the exercises.

| | |
|---|---|
| General: | White work surface, masking tape, palettes, cups, or larger mixing containers, spoons and forks for mixing, paper towels, plastic sheeting |
| Dye concentrate: | Yellow MX-8G, Yellow MX-3RA, Red MX-8B, Red MX-5B, Blue MX-G, Turquoise MX-G, and Black MX-CWNA, 1/2 cup (120 ml) each |
| Auxiliaries: | Print paste, extra-thick print paste, urea water, 2 - 3 cups (480 - 720 ml) each |
| Fabric: | Dry, soda-soaked cotton: ten 1/2 yard (meter) pieces and one yard (meter) piece |
| Tools: | Select from Painting and Printing Tools on page 25 and from the following: |

*Sponge and block printing:* thick felt, string, self-adhesive sponge products, heat-moldable foam, heat gun, water-resistant glue, thick sponges, wood and carving tools, various shapes wood blocks, sponges, rigid plastic, double-sided tape and duct tape or drawer pulls with suction cups for handles

*Silk screen printing:* self-adhesive plastic shelf paper, wax paper, freezer paper or plain paper, tape, squeegees, light-sensitive silk screen products, two or more pre-stretched blank silk screens – about 15″ x 20″ (37 cm x 50 cm)

*Rubbings:* plastic fencing, dish drainers, floor mats, textures from nature, carved wood or plastic, low-relief plastic or firm rubber shapes

*Monoprinting:* two or more rigid plastic sheets, any size from 2″ - 12″ (5 - 30 cm), dense foam sheets, rigid notched adhesive spreaders, shaped scrapers for paints and plaster, combs, textured gloves.

Additional tools used in Chapter 6. Back row from left: silkscreen with footprints made with light-sensitive product, rubber squeegee, silkscreen with key symbol made with self-adhesive shelf paper, silk screen with stone shapes cut out of paper, roll of self-adhesive shelf paper. Front from left: spiral felt block, textured sponge, leaf-shaped stamp, L-shaped sponge, fuzzy paint tool with handle, foam sheets scored with lines, sponge shape taped on rigid plastic with suction handles, wood blocks carved with router, notched adhesive spreader, dense foam roller, wood grain tool, squeegees, white dish drainer with circles, orange construction fencing, gloves with texture, double-sided tape, thick felt, dense foam sheet, heat gun, self-adhesive sponge insulation, water-resistant glue, foam blocks.

# Sponges, Single Color

Two different sponges printed alternately with thick black on dry fabric.

*See supply list on page 78. For recipes, see pages 36 - 37.*

**TIP**
Blot with a sponge or paper towel to remove excess dye without smearing it.

1. Tape down corners of 1/2 yard (meter) dry, soda-soaked cotton.
2. Prepare one or more thick colors.
3. Select sponges with cut-out shapes or interesting texture. Apply color by dipping sponge in shallow pool of color in flat tray. Turn sponge upright so excess color flows into sponge or pat color side of sponge on empty paint tray to get it to absorb color.
4. Practice printing color on fabric. It is much easier to press evenly if sponge is glued or taped to wood block or rigid plastic. If dye is applied in thick blobs that do not soak into fabric completely, you may see lighter spots in those places after fabric is washed.

Where color was applied in thick blobs, soda was not able to fix color, resulting in two washed-out spots.

OPTIONS
• Sponge print on wet, soda-soaked fabric with thick colors.
• Print repeat design with one block, creating variety by changing value and color as you move across fabric.
• Make ten combinations with same two blocks on ten pieces of fabric.

## Sponges, Multicolor

Smooth L-shaped sponge was dipped into several thickened colors on tray and printed on cotton sateen. Thin violet was painted around wet shapes and a black line was drawn with needle-tip bottle.

*See supply list on page 78. For recipes, see page 28*

1. Tape down corners of 1/2 yard (meter) dry, soda-soaked cotton.
2. Prepare several thick colors and put 1 Tbs to 2 Tbs (15 ml to 30 ml) of each on one flat tray. Do not stir.
3. Cut a thick sponge into a shape you like. Dip sponge into colors, allowing it to absorb them.
4. Print your sponge shape. If you keep the direction of sponge the same each time you dip, colors will stay in approximately the same position on sponge.
5. Refill colors in about the same arrangement as before.
6. Paint background colors with thin dyes. The thin colors will flow around printed shapes if they are applied sparingly. Where space is allowed, thin mixed colors separate on the fabric.

### OPTIONS

- Gradually rotate shape so colors print in a different place each time.
- Attach large sponge shape to piece of rigid plastic. Pour big puddles of thick colors on large tray and print.
- Use very pale thick colors to print. Paint thin dark colors in background, allowing them to flow under pale colors.

## Stamps

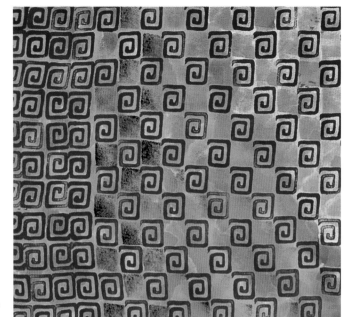

Thick red was rolled onto 3″ (7.5 cm) felt spiral glued to wood block and printed in both checkerboard and solid patterns. Thin and thick colors were applied with fuzzy sponge stamp.

*See supply list on page 78. For recipes, see pages 36 - 37.*

1. Tape down corners of 1/2 yard (meter) dry, soda-soaked cotton.
2. Prepare several colors with medium print paste.
3. Prepare a 2″ to 3″ (5 cm to 7.5 cm) stamp by attaching thick felt, self-adhesive sponge insulation, or other absorbent material to a wood block or sheet of rigid plastic.
4. Apply one color evenly on roller, then transfer color to stamp. If you choose a stamp material that is too smooth, color will not adhere well.
5. Create several patterns on same piece of fabric with your stamp.
6. Fill in background between your stamps with a gradation of colors. Paint or print one color on fabric and gradually add small amounts of a second color to first. Scatter marks you make or start on one side and work across fabric. Do not wash brush or sponge between color changes.

### OPTIONS

- Cut a potato or other raw vegetable and use it as stamp.
- Make your own stamps with heat-moldable foam products from craft suppliers.
- Make stamps with string, heavily textured fabric, or lace. Experiment with viscosity of dye, and pressure required to make distinct print.

## Blocks

Thick black printed with two wood blocks carved with machine router. Background color was sprayed on after black was dry.

A single 8" x 10" (20 cm x 25 cm) foam block with a design scored into it was printed on patterned-weave silk.

*See supply list on page 78. For recipes, see pages 36 - 37.*

1. Tape down corners of 1/2 yard (meter) dry, soda-soaked cotton.
2. Prepare several colors with print paste or medium print paste.
3. Prepare a 6" to 10" (15 cm to 25 cm) block by carving wood or by gluing string, felt, sponge, or thin foam products to wood or rigid plastic. If the block is hard to pick up, make a handle for it with duct tape or suction cups screwed to drawer pulls.
4. Apply color to block with roller.
5. Print block in one or more patterns on fabric.
6. After printed colors have dried slightly, paint or print background with thick or thin colors.

### OPTIONS

• Print on fabric that has a design woven into it.
• Paint background first and then print, either before or after it cures.
• Use one block as a background texture for another block. Change values to accentuate difference.

**T I P**
A hard stamp like a carved wood block will give a better impression if you work on a slightly padded surface or on damp fabric.

# Rubbings

Upper: plastic fence under fabric was moved several times while color was rolled on.
Lower: fence was used as a stencil on top of fabric. After dye cured, whole piece was low-water immersion dyed.

*See supply list on page 78. For recipes, see pages 36 - 37.*

1. Prepare several colors with print paste or medium print paste.
2. Place textured materials, such as a floor mat, a dish drainer or piece of bark, *under* fabric.
3. Use 1/2 yard (meter) dry, soda-soaked cotton. Take a rubbing by rolling a smooth roller coated with color on fabric over textured materials. Experiment with using different pressure on roller and different amounts and consistencies of colors.
4. Move textured materials around under fabric and create overlapped designs.
5. Fill fabric with color.

OPTIONS
• Change angle of direction of roller without changing placement of the textured material.
• Paint with more than one color on roller at a time.
• Keep eyes open for more textures – in hardware stores, housewares departments, and outdoors.

## Small Monoprints

Six different monoprints were made with a dense foam block from which color was scraped before being printed. Each print has some common lines because they were scored into foam.

*See supply list on page 78. For recipes, see pages 36 - 37.*

1. Prepare several colors with medium print paste.
2. Tape down corners of 1/2 yard (meter) dry, soda-soaked cotton.
3. Use a piece of smooth rigid plastic or a sheet of dense foam mounted on rigid plastic. Add a handle made of duct tape or suction cups screwed to drawer pull to make printing easier.
4. Select color and roll evenly onto plastic or foam block with a smooth foam roller.
5. Scrape a design in color on the block with a paint brush, notched adhesive scraper, or textured gloves.
6. Press block firmly on fabric before color gets too dry.
7. Repeat with as many variations as you can devise, filling fabric.

### OPTIONS
- Use bristle brush or another tool with texture to apply dye to block before printing.
- Roll dye on block, but not out to edges, to print a different shape.
- Roll two or more colors on block before you make the design.

### TIP
Wrinkles in the fabric will have a big impact on the final monoprint.

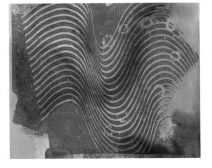

A single red monoprint with thin yellow and blue painted over it.

## Large Monoprints

A square yard (meter) of silk monoprinted with thickened dyes. Fabric was turned and printed again, making a second set of lines perpendicular to first.

*See supply list on page 78. For recipes, see pages 36 - 37.*

1. Prepare several thick colors.
2. Put 2 tsp to 3 tsp (10 ml to 15 ml) of each color on white work surface.
3. Spread and mix colors with gloved hand, brush, roller, or scraper, until you have a pattern you like.
4. Lay 1/2 yard (meter) of dry, soda-soaked cotton over colors. Gently pull and/or press out folds and bubbles. Smoothness of work surface and amount and consistency of colors will determine your results.
5. Pick up fabric and turn it over onto a piece of plastic. Allow to partly dry. If you have big blobs of color on fabric, blot some off with sponge or paper towel.
6. Spread and mix colors left on work surface. Add more if colors are depleted.
7. Monoprint another 1/2 yard (meter) of dry, soda-soaked cotton and remove from work surface.
8. Spread and mix colors and add more if necessary. Monoprint first or second piece again.

**TIP**

Colors remaining on work surface are contaminated with soda ash and will not be full strength for very long.

### OPTIONS

• Leave fabric on work surface where it was monoprinted and lay another piece of fabric over it. Press, using stamp or block to pick up excess dye coming through first piece.
• Leave colors in puddles on work surface and, after laying fabric over them, pull them with squeegee.
• Change texture of work surface to get different results.

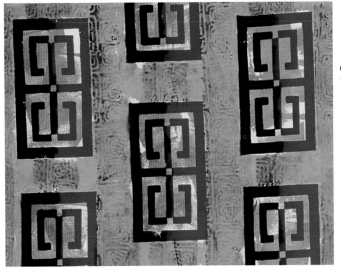

## Silk Screen, Simple

Silk screen design was made with self-adhesive plastic shelf paper. Thick black and orange were put on screen and pulled across together. Lighter value background colors were rolled on.

*See supply list on page 78. For recipes, see pages 36 - 37.*

1. Tape down corners of 1/2 yard (meter) dry, soda-soaked cotton.
2. Cut a piece of self-adhesive plastic shelf paper the size of the outside of a pre-stretched silk screen. Cut a design out of the self-adhesive plastic, removing the parts where you want the color to print through to the fabric. When you cut, allow about 3″ (7.5 cm) space all around inside edges of silk-screen frame.
3. Rub the self-adhesive paper firmly onto side of pre-stretched silk screen that will be touching fabric. Position silk screen on fabric.
4. Make batch of extra-thick print paste (page 29) and use it to make extra-thick colors.
5. Place color at inside edge of screen and pull it with squeegee across design. It takes practice to get even colors and prints without smears. The larger the screen, the more difficult to print.
6. Practice with lots of repeats using different colors. For color gradation as you work, don't wash screen between color changes.
7. When screen prints are almost dry, paint or print background with any color, any consistency.

### OPTIONS
• Cut or tear design from heavy paper and tape it to screen.
• Use roller instead of squeegee to push dye through screen.
• Put more than one color on screen before you pull squeegee.

## Silk Screen, Fine Detail

Sets of baby feet were transferred photographically to silk screen and printed on dry fabric.

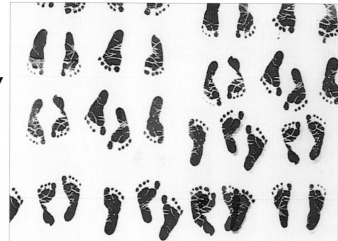

*See supply list on page 78. For recipes, see pages 36 - 37. There are several light-sensitive products for making silk-screen designs, available from art suppliers. Each has its own particular requirements – follow the manufacturer's directions.*

1. Spread light-sensitive liquid on the screen and allow it to dry in the dark.
2. For your design, create opaque black image on clear plastic. Place it tightly on silk screen and expose it to a light source, either sunlight or a light bulb, *following the product directions.* This hardens areas of design that are not covered by black. Areas under black wash out, allowing colors to print through in those places.
3. Prepare one or more extra-thick colors, made with extra-thick print paste.
4. Tape down corners of 1/2 yard (meter) dry, soda-soaked cotton. Position silk screen on top of fabric.
5. Use squeegee to push colors through screen. Print images far enough apart so that dye from fabric will not be picked up and moved around by silk screen frame. Accurate screen printing is a skill that takes experience, but with just a little practice you can achieve very good results.

### OPTIONS
- Read about making your own silk screens, or take a workshop. Most silk screen techniques work with thickened Procion®MX dyes.
- Look up silk-screen businesses in your area. Price their services: building and stretching screens; making transparencies from your images; putting images onto screens.
- Prepare padded table with washable surface like white vinyl and practice using large silk screens.

**TIP**
Some light-sensitive products contain toxic chemicals, so avoid contact with the skin and any chance of ingestion.

Sponges, stamps, blocks and silk screens offer unlimited potential for exploring line and shape. Changes in value, color, angle, and placement change the visual impact of the print. When printing techniques are added to brush and roller work, you can increase the complexity of the design. Remember to work with various consistencies of colors to fit the tools you use and the results you wish to see.

## Combine Print Techniques

Key lock shape was screened on dry, wrinkled fabric in a random arrangement, changing color with each print. Thin colors were painted on immediately, and while still wet, thickened black was drawn with a pointed bottle.

## Combine
## Print
## Techniques
*continued*

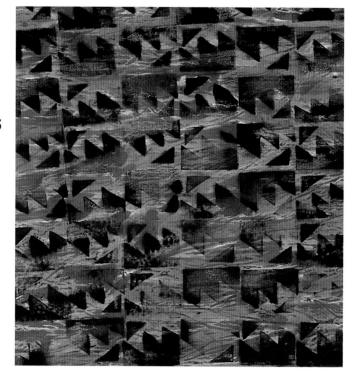

Thick red was monoprinted on dry cotton, then thin, pale yellow was painted over. While wet, thick black was printed in repeat pattern with large sponge block.

*See supply list on page 78. For recipes, see pages 36 - 37.*

1. Prepare several thick colors and spread them around on the work surface.
2. Monoprint 1 yard (meter) of dry, soda-soaked cotton.
3. Turn fabric over onto plastic.
4. Use stamp or block to print over the monoprint, either while it is still wet or when it is almost dry.
5. Decide what to do with any background you may have left. Paint with thin colors and let them spread or use thick colors to print more blocks or paint in colors.

OPTIONS

• Use a textured sponge and thick or medium-consistency colors to roll over stencil or masked design. Remove stencil or masked shapes and use a block to print another pattern on top of first colors.
• Use a rubbing from textured surface as background for detailed silk screen design. Do either layer first.
• Start developing collection of home-made stamps, blocks, and screens for printing with Procion®MX dyes.

## Combine Print Techniques
*continued*

An 8″ x 10″ (20 cm x 25 cm) block of smooth, dense foam was first scored with a pen. Then it was coated evenly with thick black and a wood grain tool was rocked and pulled the length of the block three times, creating different marks. After black cured, thin colors were painted over the whole piece.

# WATER-SOLUBLE RESISTS

Water-soluble resists can be combined with the use of thickened dyes to create negative images on the fabric. The tremendous advantage of using resists that are water-soluble is that they wash out with the excess dye; they do not require special solvents or processes to be removed completely. Dye concentrate mixed with print paste will not dissolve them. Even thin colors painted on lightly will be resisted by most of these products. Of course, water-soluble resists are not practical for any kind of immersion dyeing, because the resist will dissolve in the dye-bath.

There are many kinds of water-soluble resists available, and they all work differently. Some pre-made products work very well, penetrating the fabric completely and preventing any color penetration from above or below. Others prevent the flow of the dye through the fibers, but when color is painted over them, they act only as a partial resist. Some are very thick and the easiest to brush on; others are a good consistency for squeezing out of a needle-tip bottle.

There are also various food products like starches and sugars that can be cooked and used on the fabric to resist thickened dyes. These products vary greatly in how much they spread or resist and in how hard they are to wash out of the fabric. Two that work particularly well are corn dextrin and potato dextrin. Corn dextrin will stay liquid when cool, so it can be brushed on or applied in fine lines that will not crack. Potato dextrin cools to a firm paste consistency and when applied in a heavy layer, cracks all over as it dries.

A resist was squeezed from a pointed bottle onto dry fabric. While it was drying, thick black lines were drawn with needle-tip bottle. Upper part: thin dark tan was painted on while black was still wet. Lower: lighter color was painted after black had almost dried.

Two pre-made resists on dry, soda-soaked fabric. One flowed easily through a pointed bottle. The other, which was more viscous, making blobs, did not resist the penetration of the colors as much as the first.

## SUPPLY LIST / CHAPTER 7

Have the following at hand before you begin the exercises.

| | |
|---|---|
| General: | White work surface, masking tape, palettes, cups, or larger mixing containers, spoons and forks for mixing, paper towels, plastic sheeting, saucepan with lid, whisk, measuring cups for liquid and dry ingredients, burner for cooking |
| Dye concentrate: | Yellow MX-8G, Red MX-8B, Blue MX-G, and Black MX-CWNA, 1/2 cup (120 ml) each |
| Auxiliaries: | Soda solution, print paste and urea water, 2 - 3 cups (480 - 720 ml) each |
| | Cooked resists: Powdered corn dextrin and powdered potato dextrin, 1 lb (455 g) each |
| | Pre-made resists: Silkpaint Water-Soluble Resist, Elmer's Glue Gel, glue stick, Ungutta, Presist, Casava Paste, Inkodye Resist, any others – chose two or more |
| Fabric: | Dry, soda-soaked cotton: 4 fat quarters and two 1/2 yard (meter) pieces |
| Tools: | Needle-tip bottle, bristle brush, textured sponge, sponge block, stamp, rigid notched scraper, rigid spatula or putty knife |

Additional items used for fabrics in Chapter 7. From left, back: Jacquard Water-Based Resist, Silkpaint Water-Soluble Resist, Elmer's Glue Gel, glue sticks, Ungutta, needle-tip bottle of Ungutta, Presist, needle-tip bottle of Presist. Foreground from left: powdered corn dextrin, cooked corn dextrin, saucepan and whisk, cooked potato dextrin, powdered potato dextrin, smooth and notched scrapers, plastic putty knife, bristle brushes, sponge with parallel ridges.

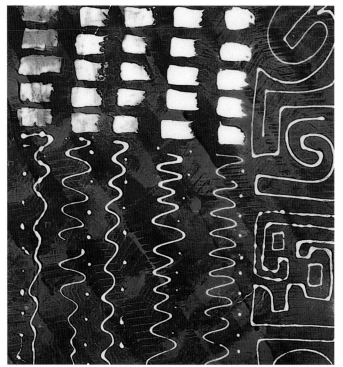

## Pre-Made Resists

Five pre-made water-soluble resists. See wide brush marks, left to right: Jacquard Water-based Resist; Silkpaint Water-soluble Resist; Elmer's Glue Gel; Ungutta; Presist

*See supply list on page 94. For recipes, see pages 36 - 37.*

1. Tape down corners of 1/2 yard (meter) dry, soda-soaked cotton.
2. Select two or more pre-made water-soluble resists and apply them to dry fabric, brushing, stamping, and squeezing them out of needle-tip bottle. Observe which resists flow on fabric the way you like.
3. Allow fabric to dry completely.
4. Prepare several colors with print paste or medium print paste. If your colors are very thin, they may dissolve the resist.
5. Paint or print colors over dry resists. Do not cover fabric with plastic until it is almost dry, because the wetness may dissolve the resist at edges.
6. Cure and wash fabric to determine which ones resist the most or leave a texture.

### OPTIONS
• Try other glue or starch products that are water-soluble. You may find one that is better, cheaper, or easier to get. Be sure they wash out easily.
• Find a water-soluble resist that will not dissolve too much when thin colors are applied over it.

**TIP**
Some resists need to be applied very thickly to leave completely white fabric underneath.

## COOKED RESIST RECIPES

Corn and potato dextrin have various uses in the food industry, such as thickening and sweetening. Corn dextrin is a yellow powder that, when cooked as described on the next page, will remain a semi-thick, opaque liquid at room temperature. It can completely resist the penetration of thickened colors and washes out easily in water. Potato dextrin is a white powder that becomes a clear liquid when dissolved in boiling water. As it cools to room temperature, it becomes opaque and firm, and when spread thickly on fabric, it cracks as it dries.

Cold potato dextrin made without soda on white cotton. Lines were scraped in wet dextrin with notched spreader. When dry, thick black was rolled over all. Areas of less contrast often occurs when no soda is added to the dextrin (see left edge).

There are many recipes for cooking corn and potato dextrin resists. The recipes that follow are those that I have found work the most often for me. Many things influence the results: the humidity, the heat of the burner, the length of boiling, and the thickness of application. The products also can vary, so the recipes should be used as guides to experiment and adjust as needed.

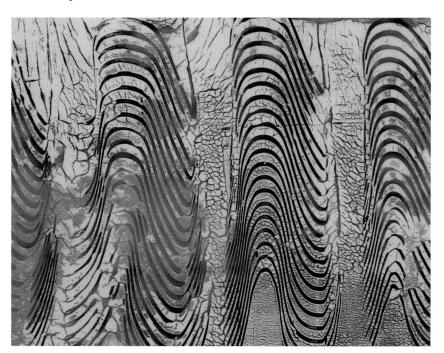

## RECIPE FOR CORN DEXTRIN

1 cup (240 ml) water

1 1/4 cup (300 ml) powdered corn dextrin

When water starts to boil, add corn dextrin, stir with whisk until lumps are gone. Simmer for 5 to 8 minutes. Cool to room temperature with a cover to minimize crust. It spreads much more on the fabric if you use it hot or warm. Cooked this way, corn dextrin does not crack when it dries. If you find that the color penetrates the corn dextrin, it may need to be spread on thicker or cooked slightly longer. Note that if it turns crystalline when it cools, it has been cooked too long and may cut threads of the fabric when it is folded. It should be stored cool and can be used as long as you can spread it.

## RECIPE FOR POTATO DEXTRIN

1 cup (240 ml) soda solution (see recipe page 36)

1 cup (240 ml) powdered potato dextrin

When soda water starts to boil, add potato dextrin, stir with whisk over heat until lumps are gone – 2 to 5 minutes. Then simmer 5 minutes. The mixture turns gold because of soda. Use hot, which is transparent and runny; warm, which is thicker; or room temperature, which will be firm and opaque. Cool to room temperature with cover to minimize crust. Potato dextrin cracks as it dries; how thickly it is applied determines the size of the cracks. Thickened dye penetrates only through the cracks and places where the dextrin is spread very thinly. It should be stored cool and can be used as long as you can spread it.

## Corn Dextrin

Cold corn dextrin applied with bristle brush to white fabric. Thick colors were brushed on over dry dextrin. The dextrin dissolves when fabric is washed.

*See supply list on page 94. For recipes, see pages 36 - 37.*

1. Tape down corners of fat quarter of dry, soda-soaked cotton.
2. Prepare corn dextrin according to recipe (page 97) and cool to room temperature.
3. Paint or draw cooked corn dextrin in patterns and shapes on fabric.
4. Let corn dextrin dry completely.
5. Mix thick colors and paint them over resist.
6. Cure and wash as usual.

OPTIONS
- Use stamps or textured sponges to apply corn dextrin.
- Put corn dextrin on a light-colored fabric that has been soda-soaked and dried. Then apply another layer of thick colors.
- Put some dye concentrate in corn dextrin before painting it on fabric. Allow to dry slowly and then apply more thickened colors.

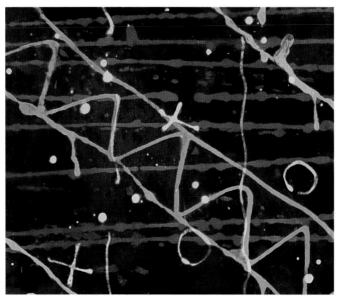

## Corn Dextrin in Layers

Corn dextrin and thickened colors were applied in layers on fabric, starting with dots and circles on white, then diagonal lines on yellow, then horizontal lines on red, then black as top layer.

*See supply list on page 94. For recipes, see pages 36 - 37.*

1. Tape down corners of fat quarter of dry, soda-soaked cotton.
2. Prepare corn dextrin according to recipe (page 97) and cool to room temperature.
3. Apply cooked corn dextrin in patterns on fabric.
4. Prepare three medium-thin colors, light to dark values. When I am applying many layers of color, I use a thinner print paste, because thick layers will prevent some penetration of the colors. If medium-thin color is applied sparingly, it will not dissolve corn dextrin.
5. Using brush or roller, apply a pale value of a medium-thin color over dry dextrin.
6. When the color is almost dry, apply corn dextrin again and let fabric cure four hours, then dry completely.
7. Repeat with another layer of corn dextrin and darker value color than first. Cure and dry.
8. Repeat with another layer of corn dextrin and darker value color. Cure and wash.

### OPTIONS
• Start with light colored fabric (soda-soaked).
• Use more than one kind of tool to apply dextrin and colors.
• Do layers once with extreme value changes and once with more subtle contrast in values.

**T I P**

Painting layers of color and dextrin could take two or more days, depending on humidity, number of layers, viscosity, and amount of dye applied at each layer.

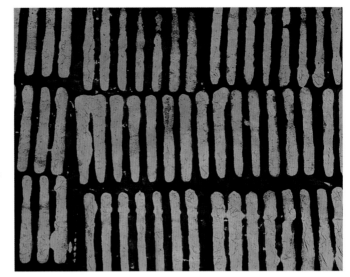

## Potato Dextrin, Hot

Hot potato dextrin printed on light blue fabric with ridged sponge. Thick maroon was applied with roller.

*See supply list on page 94. For recipes, see pages 36 - 37.*

1. Prepare potato dextrin (page 97).
2. Tape down corners of fat quarter dry, soda-soaked cotton.
3. While dextrin is still hot, pour some into flat tray and use textured sponge to print it on fabric. As dextrin cools and dries it will shrink and crack, pulling fabric away from tape. If you can keep edges of fabric from rolling, it will be easier to apply color later.
4. Allow to dry completely.
5. Prepare one color with medium print paste.
6. Using brush or roller, paint color into all cracks in dextrin.
7. Do not cover fabric with plastic during curing time unless you see that it might dry out completely.

**TIP**

Even though the potato dextrin has soda solution in it, fabric should also have soda solution on it.

Hot potato dextrin applied with brush on white fabric. Places where it was thickest had most resist and largest cracks.

### OPTIONS

- Use medium-thin color and cover fabric during the cure time.
- Keep fabric taped to same board through whole process, including spraying dextrin off with a hose outside.

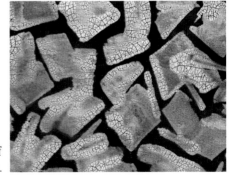

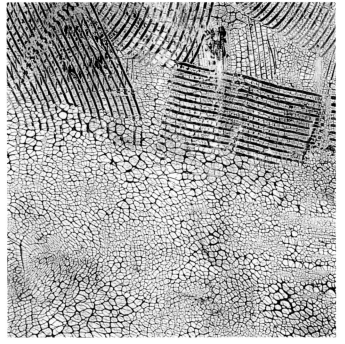

## Potato Dextrin, Cold

Cotton covered with cold potato dextrin made with soda. Thickened color applied evenly over top with a roller. Were the dextrin is applied thinly, the cracks are smaller.

*See supply list on page 94. For recipes, see pages 36 - 37.*

1. Tape down corners of fat quarter dry, soda-soaked cotton.
2. Prepare potato dextrin according to recipe (page 97) and allow to cool to room temperature. Use stiff plastic putty knife or spatula to spread dextrin either all over fabric or leaving spaces. It may be very stiff, but can be spread if you press hard and pull.
3. Dry completely. Larger chunks may fall off as it dries, but that will make an even more interesting texture.
4. Prepare one color with medium print paste and spread it over the dextrin with brush or roller. Make sure you don't just skim over top of dextrin which may have curled or warped as it dried, but get color into cracks so it can contact fabric.
5. Do not cover fabric with plastic during the curing time unless you see that it might dry out completely.

### OPTIONS
• Scrape into potato dextrin with notched tool or stick before it dries.
• Use more than one color to paint after potato dextrin has dried.
• Spread potato dextrin over already dyed fabric (soda-soaked).

**TIP**

For a yard (meter) of fabric, you may need two or three times the recipe on page 97.

## Combine Resist Techniques

Water-soluble resists are a simple way to put a negative image on fabric, giving it a different kind of interest than a positive image has. Pre-made resists are quick and easy, corn dextrin is very versatile as a liquid, and potato dextrin gives a crackle effect that cannot be duplicated. These resists can be combined with each other and other printing techniques to produce endless variety in textile designs.

Cotton painted and printed in multiple layers, cured and dried, then painted with both corn and potato dextrin before being covered with colors again.

## Combine Resist Techniques
*continued*

Corn dextrin brushed and squeezed from a pointed bottle over stamped and painted cotton, then dark colors rolled on.

## Combine Resist Techniques
*continued*

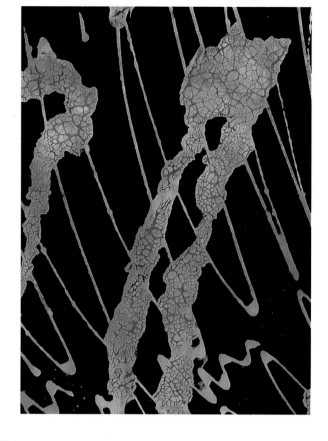

Corn dextrin was applied with needle-tip bottle on gold fabric (soda-soaked). Then, warm potato dextrin without soda was squirted on in wide lines. After fabric dried, thickened black was rolled over.

*See supply list on page 94. For recipes, see pages 36 - 37.*

1. Prepare corn and potato dextrin according to recipes (page 97).
2. Tape down corners of 1/2 yard (meter) dry, soda-soaked cotton.
3. Apply both corn and potato dextrin on the fabric with various tools and allow them to dry.
4. Prepare one or more colors with medium print paste.
5. Paint or roll the colors onto the fabric. Cure and wash.

### OPTIONS

- Apply corn dextrin to fabric. Dry, then apply a color. Cure and dry. Apply potato dextrin. Dry, then apply another color.
- Paint fabric with a pale color. Cure and dry. Then apply cold corn dextrin and hot or cold potato dextrin. Dry, apply another color.
- Mix potato and corn dextrin. Is mixture easier to spread than potato dextrin alone? How much crackle do you get?

## Combine Resist Techniques
*continued*

A grid was placed under white fabric. Potato dextrin was spread with wide putty knife, pushing it down into grid. Upper left, plastic construction fence was placed between grid and fabric when dextrin was scraped on. Three colors were painted over. Very dark area shows where there was no potato dextrin.

# LAYERS OF COLORS

The more layers of color you apply to the fabric, the more difficult it is to predict what the results will be. However, it is helpful to remember that the first dye to penetrate the fabric will have the most impact. There will be more places for the dye to bond and less print paste on the fabric to dilute the colors or prevent their full penetration to the fabric. A very pale, thick color under a dark color will show up more than if it is put on top.

The exercises in this chapter are designed to help you see the differences between painting on a dry layer of color and a wet layer, and between painting on a wet layer of thick colors and painting on a wet layer of thin colors. As you paint or print one color over another, you will gain experience with how transparent colors mix visually. A simple alternative for overlapping colors is to paint and print on a piece of fabric, cure, low-water immersion dye it, then wash it. And of course, the use of water-soluble resists over and under your colors will expand the possibilities and add complexity to your fabric designs. When the fabric is all dyed and washed, there is always the possibility of painting or printing on it again – after it is soda-soaked.

Dry cotton mono-printed with thick colors and hung up to drip. Corn dextrin spread in irregular shapes over whole piece and dried. Then thick black dye was rolled on.

## SUPPLY LIST / CHAPTER 8

Have the following at hand before you begin the exercises.

| | |
|---|---|
| General: | White work surface, masking tape, palettes, cups, or larger mixing containers, spoons and forks for mixing, paper towels, plastic sheeting |
| Dye concentrate: | Yellow MX-8G, Yellow MX-3RA, Red MX-8B, Red MX-5B, Blue MX-G, Turquoise MX-G and Black MX-CWNA, 1 cup (240 ml) each |
| Auxiliaries: | Soda solution, 2 cups (480 ml) |
| | Print paste, urea water, 4 cups (960 ml) each |
| | Extra-thick print paste, 2 cups (480 ml) |
| | Water-soluble resists (choose from list on page 94), amount optional |
| Fabric: | Dry, soda-soaked cotton: seven 1 yard (meter) pieces |
| | Cotton without soda: 1 yard (meter) piece |
| | Silk without soda: 1 yard (meter) piece |
| Tools: | Your favorite painting and printing tools, brushes, stamps, textures, screens, shapes, squeeze bottles, and any other tools you devise |

Additional tools used for fabrics illustrated in Chapter 8. Back row, from left: foam insulation strips on rigid plastic, hand-cut sponge shape on rigid plastic with suction handle on back, large packing sponge with circular and linear cut-outs, x-shaped sponge glued to sponge backing. Foreground from left: notched sponge brush, large bristle brush, white dish drainer, orange paint tray liner, blue heat-molded dense foam block, round sponge on rigid plastic, roll of masking tape dots.

## Two Layers, Thick

Rigid plastic with sponge strips made blocks of black lines. While wet, a roller dipped in several colors was used to fill background. Detail shows impression made on roller by texture of the paint tray.

*See supply list on page 108. For recipes, see pages 36 - 37.*

1. Tape corners of 1 yard (meter) dry, soda-soaked cotton to work surface.
2. Prepare several colors with print paste or medium print paste.
3. Cover fabric with colors using large block from your collection. By the time you are finished printing, some parts may be almost dry.
4. Without waiting for fabric to dry further, use brush and/or roller to apply second layer of color. Roller may pick up some color where there were blobs and print it as it rolls. Paint brush can place color more particularly, but might smear colors where they are still thick and wet.

### OPTIONS

• Cover fabric with negative shapes made with impressions on the roller. Then paint several medium-thin colors over all.

• Draw line design all over fabric. While it is wet, paint marks over half of it. Wait for other half to almost dry and paint same marks.

• Take rubbing from textured surface such as a door mat, moving it to fill whole piece. Let colors get dry to touch, then take another rubbing from another texture.

## Two Layers, Thick/Thin

Thick colors mono-
printed from work
surface. After colors
dried, thin green
and aqua were
painted in spaces.

*See supply list on page 108. For recipes, see pages 36 - 37.*

Large sponge dipped
in a tray of thick
gold, red, and blue,
unmixed. Thin
yellow and aqua
were painted over
the prints while they
were still wet.

1. Prepare several extra-thick colors and several thin colors.
2. Use extra-thick colors to monoprint 1 yard (meter) dry, soda-soaked cotton.
3. Turn fabric over onto plastic.
4. Without waiting for colors to dry on half of fabric, paint generous amounts of thin colors in and around monoprint.
5. Wait for other half to feel almost dry and then paint thin colors in background spaces.

OPTIONS
• Draw line design with thick colors. Then paint thin colors over them, pulling and smearing lines.
• Do monoprint with thick colors and paint thin colors on back of fabric.

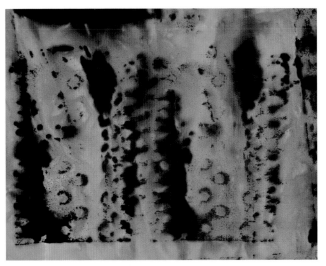

## Two Layers, Thin/Thick

Detail of fabric painted with thin yellow. Before it dried, a roller with thick black dye was pressed on dotted paint tray and applied to fabric.

*See supply list on page 108. For recipes, see pages 36 - 37.*

1. Prepare one or more thick colors and one or more thin colors.
2. Spread thin colors on the whole 1 yard (meter) dry, soda-soaked cotton with roller or wide paint brush. If you leave spaces between places you put colors, they will migrate and separate, creating a halo effect.
3. While still wet, apply thick colors with stamps, rollers, or brushes on half of fabric.
4. Wait for other half to get dry to touch and apply same marks.

Detail of photo on page 146. After thin background colors were cured and dry, thick black was printed with sponge.

### OPTIONS
• Work on wet, soda-soaked fabric with thin colors and allow them to spread before printing with thick colors.
• Use a very dense fabric like cotton velveteen or heavy raw silk for the same exercise.

# Three Layers, Thick

A grid was placed under dry silk and roller was used to make a rubbing. After colors dried, diamond-shaped grid and spirals were printed. Then large leaves and ferns were used as mask and thick colors were rolled over them.

*See supply list on page 108. For recipes, see pages 36 - 37.*

1. Prepare thick dyes and monoprint 1 yard (meter) dry, soda-soaked cotton.
2. Turn it over or hang it up to get almost dry.
3. Apply lines with thick colors in needle-tip bottles or on brushes or rollers. Use lines to accent or contrast with first layer of color.
4. Allow it to get almost dry again.
5. Apply mask of some kind (tape, leaves, or cut-out shelf paper shapes).
6. Roll thick or medium-consistency colors over the masked areas.

### OPTIONS

• Use silk with decorative weave for this exercise.
• Monoprint fabric with a scant amount of thick color, so surface is fairly dry. Paint thick colors over monoprint and while it is still wet, print a block or other stamp as third layer of design.
• Print an all-over design by taking rubbing from a texture. Almost dry, then mask and paint with thick colors. Remove mask and either before or after it is almost dry, paint with roller impressions.

### TIP

If you want to go on with more layers, you should consider washing it and soda-soaking the fabric again.

## Two Layers, Wet

Black roller impressions and pale gray brush marks were put on wet, soda-soaked cotton. Medium-thin gold was rolled across while it was wet, then thin yellow was brushed in spaces.

*See supply list on page 108. For recipes, see page 36 - 37.*

1. Dunk 1 yard (meter) cotton (without soda) in soda solution; wring out and place on work surface.
2. Paint or print thick colors on wet fabric, leaving spaces.
3. Prepare more colors, with print paste or medium print paste.
4. Apply them over parts of first layer, still leaving some white spaces.
5. Fill some or all of the spaces with thin colors while fabric is still wet. Leave spaces between if you like the halo effect.
6. Cure covered to encourage flow of colors. If you wish, leave uncovered, so colors will dry more quickly and spread less.

### OPTIONS
• Paint thin colors on wet fabric, leaving lots of space between marks. After they have spread, add more marks with thick colors. Prepare some colors using only dye concentrate (no urea water, no print paste) and paint sparingly over some of the other colors.
• Monoprint with thick colors on wet fabric. Turn it over and paint thin dyes in spaces. Then add thick colors for accent while it is still wet.
• Use sponge brush to draw lines with thick color on wet fabric. Paint over and around them with medium-thin colors. Fill any spaces with thin colors.

## Three Layers, Dry/Wet

Large sponge shape was dipped into tray of thick blue and orange, unmixed. While prints were still wet, thin gold, orange, and light blue were applied. A needle-tip bottle was used to make pairs of narrow lines while silk was wet.

*See supply list on page 108. For recipes, see page 36 - 37.*

1. Prepare several thick, dark colors and several thin, pale colors.
2. Use a large block to print thick colors on 1 yard (meter) dry, soda-soaked cotton. Apply colors generously.
3. Press a sponge brush filled with thin colors around printed shapes without actually painting over them. Thin colors will flow around and under thick colors. Let them spread and blend together.
4. Print or paint another design with thick colors over whole piece while it is still wet.

### OPTIONS

- Use textured sponge to make marks with thick colors. Roll over this with medium-consistency colors. Print another shape on top while wet.
- Mask out shapes on dry fabric and use pale values of thick colors on roller with texture to fill in background. Remove mask and use thin colors to paint shapes. While wet, add accents with thick colors.
- Place dry fabric over texture. Make a rubbing. Let cure for 30 minutes, then paint thin colors. While wet, print a block with thick color.

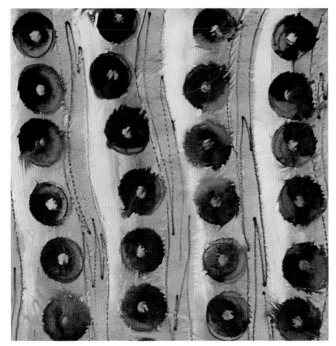

## Four Layers, Wet

Wide lines mono-
printed on wet silk.
Thin dyes were
painted between
lines. A circular
sponge was saturat-
ed with colors and
printed in rows.
While still wet,
black lines were
made with needle-
tip bottle.

*See supply list on page 108. For recipes, see pages 36 - 37.*

1. Soak 1 yard (meter) silk (without soda) in soda solution and wring out.
2. Brush thick colors in large shapes on work surface.
3. Lay wet silk on colors and let them soak in and spread. Pull edges to remove wrinkles. Pull harder to pull and smear colors, if you wish.
4. Let silk get partly dry and turn it over. Decide which side you like best and leave that side facing up.
5. Paint thin colors in spaces.
6. Paint or print over with thick colors while still wet.
7. Add accents with thick color on a stamp or block or in a needle-tip bottle.

### OPTIONS

• Rip freezer paper and place on wet fabric, wax side up. Roll thick dye over paper with textured roller. Remove paper. Add accent lines with thick colors and then paint thin color in spaces. Repeat paper and roller.
• Use thick colors to make roller impressions. Paint thin colors in back-ground. Then use needle-tip bottle to add lines. While wet, use large block to print over whole piece.
• Take rubbing on wet fabric. Let dry slightly and use roller with impres-sions on it. Stamp over other areas and fill with thin colors.

## Combine with Immersion

Overlapping prints of large silk screen with stone shapes. Black in needle-tip bottle was used for narrow lines. After curing, fabric was low-water immersion dyed.

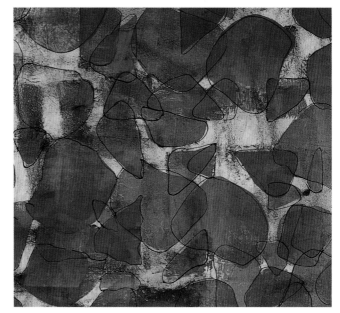

*See supply list on page 108. For recipes, see pages 36 - 37.*

1. Silk screen bold design on 1 yard (meter) dry, soda-soaked cotton, leaving a lot of white spaces.
2. Cure fabric for two or more hours. It does not have to be dry. Do not wash fabric.
3. Dye the silk screened fabric a medium or light value in low-water immersion dye bath. Follow instructions in Chapter 11 on page 139. Even though there is already soda on fabric, you should add it again because it will be diluted by the two cups (480 ml) of added liquid.
4. Allow to cure one hour as for low-water immersion dyeing.

### OPTIONS

• Monoprint large shapes with thick colors, leaving some white spaces. Cure two or more hours, then low-water immersion dye (Chapter 11, page 139), pouring different colors on each end.
• Paint thin colors on dry fabric, allowing them to separate. Cure two or more hours, then low-water immersion dye the fabric, (Chapter 11, page 139), pouring a dark color on one end and a light color on the other.
• Draw fine lines with thick dye on dry, soda-soaked fabric. Cure two or more hours, then fold fabric in a shallow tray. Pour enough soda solution over to wet it entirely, then pour on two or three colors mixed with dye concentrate only (no print paste or urea water or plain water).

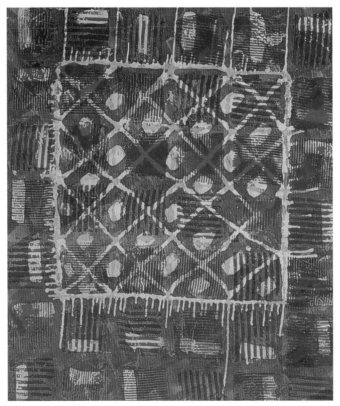

## Combine Layers with Resists

Parallel red lines were monoprinted on white cotton sateen all at once on large table. Then fabric was low-water immersion dyed gold. It was washed, dried, soaked in soda again, dried, painted with corn dextrin, dried. Thick rust and red-orange were applied with a roller.

*See supply list on page 108. For recipes, see pages 36 - 37.*

1. Choose 1 yard (meter) fabric you have painted or printed that is dry but still has soda in it.
2. Paint or print corn dextrin, Presist, or another liquid water-soluble resist in large shapes on fabric.
3. Allow resist to dry completely.
4. Roll thick color over whole piece.

### OPTIONS

• Use several different colors when you are painting over resist.
• Choose fabric that has already been washed and dried. Soda-soak and dry it. Then paint with one of the resists (page 97), dry, and paint over with a thickened color.
• Piece several blocks of fabric together, soda-soak and dry, then paint selected parts with any water-soluble resist. When it is dry, roll one or more colors onto fabric.

# LARGE-SCALE APPLICATIONS

Large pieces of fabric are often harder to paint or print than small pieces, partly because of complications caused by the larger scale: you need to mix a lot of dye and print paste, you have to work on a large surface, and you have to lift, move, and cure large pieces of fabric. Also, design composition on larger pieces offers more choices and is more likely to be subject to "accidents." If you haven't worked on large pieces of fabric, you are missing out on the fun. The fabrics shown here illustrate various combinations of techniques used in the exercises, worked at a larger scale. When you're ready, try working on 2-yard or 4-yard (meter) pieces; it's hard work, but exciting.

*Pull 2,* cotton sateen, detail. Monoprint, squeegee used on back of fabric to pull colors that had been placed underneath on the work surface.

*Spirals 2,* silk broadcloth, 70″ x 44″ (175 cm x 110 cm). Spiral shapes made by taking rubbing from a spiral form. Thin colors were immediately painted in background.

*Spirals 3,* cotton sateen, 55″ x 55″ (137 cm x 137 cm). Large spirals monoprinted, then thin gold painted on. Wood block spirals printed while wet.

*Grid 1,* cotton broadcloth, 66″ x 45″ (165 cm x 113 cm). Rubbings were made on wet fabric over plastic grid. Repetition and changing pressure created values.

*Grid 3,* silk broadcloth, 70″ x 44″ (175 cm x 110 cm). Lines monoprinted from dye on plastic grid. Background colors monoprinted and rolled on afterward.

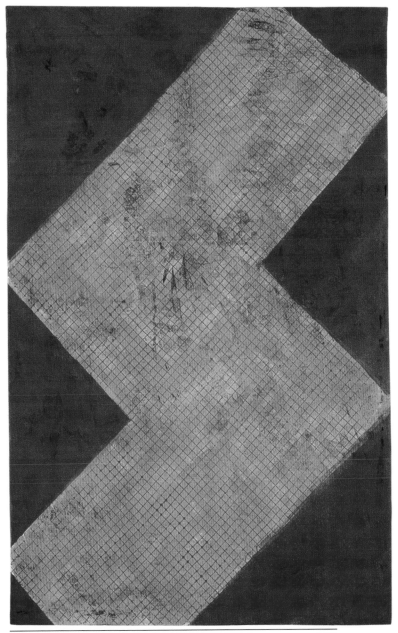

*Grid 5,* silk broadcloth, 70″ x 44″ (175 cm x 110 cm). Rubbing from plastic grid underneath. As fabric was shifted, colors were added and pressure on roller changed.

*Lines 3,* silk broadcloth, 70″ x 44″ (175 cm x 110 cm). Lines and background colors were monoprinted from work surface. Thick colors painted over afterward.

*Lines 4,* cotton sateen, 75″ x 55″ (187 cm x 137 cm). Darkest color was monoprinted from work surface. Thick gold and blue were painted on later.

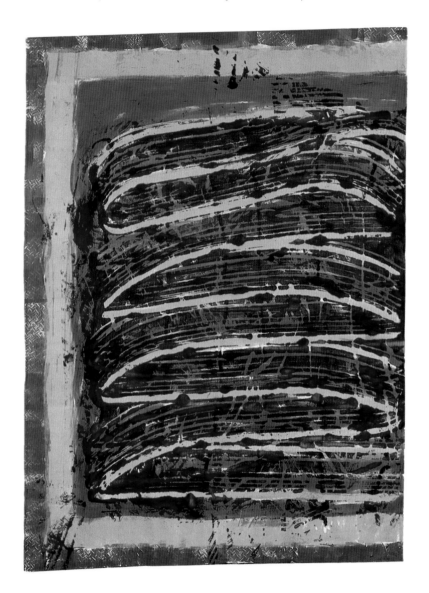

*Circles 3*, cotton sateen, 75″ x 55″ (187 cm x 137 cm). Spiral design monoprinted. Background added with rubbing over grid, roller impressions and low-water immersion.

*Dots 2,* silk broadcloth, 70″ x 44″ (170 cm x 110 cm). Thick colors were lifted from tray and printed with large sponge. Thin colors were applied with sponge brushes.

*Pull 4*, silk broadcloth, 70″ x 44″ (170 cm x 110 cm). Monoprint of thick colors poured on work surface, and pulled with notched squeegee.

# Extend Your Understanding

## PART III

Hand painting and printing color on fabric has unlimited possibilities. As you gain understanding, many, many options will open up for you. In the chapters that follow, you will learn how to dye with black mixes. You will discover the tremendous range of effects possible with low-water immersion dyeing, and how to vat dye large amounts of fabric. Alternate recipes for using Procion®MX dyes for surface applications will extend your range even further. Use this part of *Color by Design* as a resource for ideas — very soon you will be able to adapt your use of the dyes to exactly fit the needs of your projects.

*Lines 2,* cotton sateen, detail. Wavy lines and columns were monoprinted, then blue and red areas were painted with thick colors using sponge brush.

# 10

# ABOUT BLACK

Black is a difficult color to dye, for several reasons. The quality of a color is very subjective – what color is black? Is it warm or cool, does it lean towards red or green or blue? Also, black is a very dark color – it requires a lot of dye in the fiber to look black. If it is not very dark, it is not a black, but a gray. When I dye black, I prepare the dye concentrate with twice as much dye powder as I use for other colors. In order to paint a very dark black, I combine the dye concentrate with print paste to the ratio of two to one, instead of one to one as the other colors. For low-water immersion dyeing, I use more dye concentrate than I would for other dark colors and I add soda solution two times, about 10 minutes apart, to the dye-bath to be sure to maximize the amount of dye that fixes on the fabric.

Lines were made with Presist on white cotton velveteen. Two colors of thick black, one greenish, one bluish, were rolled over dry resist.

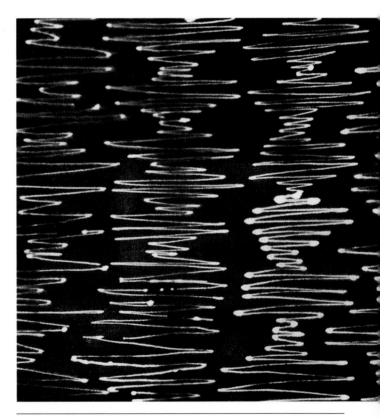

## BLACK MX-CWNA

All Procion®MX blacks are mixed from some combination of single-chemical colors (page 16). Black MX-CWNA is mixed by the manufacturer and resold under different company names. It is reformulated from time to time. Many other blacks are also mixed by individual companies and sold under their own names. Each mix results in different colors of black, depending on the colors blended to make it.

Each black mix will have different results on different fibers for the same reason. When used for low-water immersion dyeing, Black MX-CWNA in these photos appears redder on silk than on

Black MX-CWNA used in low-water immersion dye bath on cotton (left) and silk (right). Resulting colors of black are different because of nature of different fibers. Both pieces were dyed with same amount of dye concentrate in same low-water recipe.

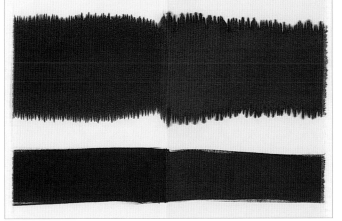

Black MX-CWNA was painted on dry cotton (left) and silk (right). Upper strip used two parts dye concentrate (double-strength) and one part urea water. Lower strip used two parts dye concentrate (double-strength) and one part print paste.

cotton, because silk reacts slightly differently to the colors than does cotton. When Black MX-CWNA is painted on cotton and silk, the same difference is easily visible, particularly where the dye is not thickened with print paste. The single-chemical colors flow through the fibers at various rates, depending on the fiber, and the resulting halo effect is a different color on silk than it is on cotton. When dye concentrate is thickened with print paste, the colors do not flow away from the painted line and the resulting concentration of color appears darker black.

## OTHER BLACK MIXES

Dharma Black 44 (left) and Pro Black 602A (right) used in low-water immersion dye-bath on cotton (top) and silk (bottom). All four pieces were dyed with same amount of dye concentrate in same low-water immersion recipe.

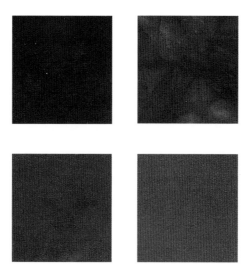

The two mixes shown here do not separate on the fabric the same as Black MX-CWNA, because they are made with a different mix of single-chemical colors. When they are low-water immersion dyed, the cotton samples are different colors of black than the silks. When these black mixes are painted, the results are very different than they would be with MX-CWNA. The thin black separates on the cotton and silk, leaving a red cast to the center and a bluish halo. The thick blacks do not separate and appear much darker.

Different Procion®MX black mixes are available from different dye suppliers, and more will undoubtedly be formulated in the future. It is important to realize that the color cast a black mix

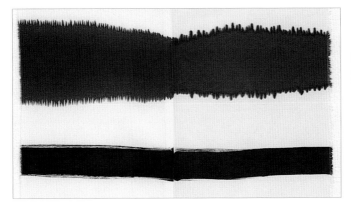

PRO Black 602A
painted on cotton
(left) and silk (right).

gives to the fabric can be changed by adding more of another color. If the black mix is very blue, Orange MX-2R can be added to it to warm it up and make it more of a neutral color. Likewise, some combination of red and yellow might be added. If the results of a black mix are too red, add the complement – green – which is some combination of blue and yellow dyes; if it is too greenish, add red or red and blue. It is not difficult to change a black mix to be the color black you prefer.

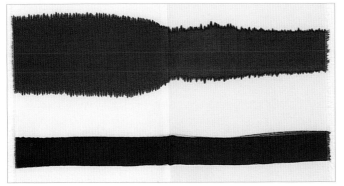

Dharma Black 44
painted on cotton
(left) and silk (right).

# ALTERNATIVE METHODS

Procion®MX dyes are extremely versatile. They can be used for immersion dyeing as well as for surface applications. Immersion dyeing is a good choice when large areas of color are the goal, and no specific design is required. The immersion process is quick and fun and combines easily with painting and printing because *identical dye concentrates and soda solution can be used.*

There are a few alternative recipes for surface applications of Procion®MX dyes which may be useful for some projects. There is a special recipe for silk only, a method to add the alkali to the colors you mix, and a method that uses steam to cure the fabric.

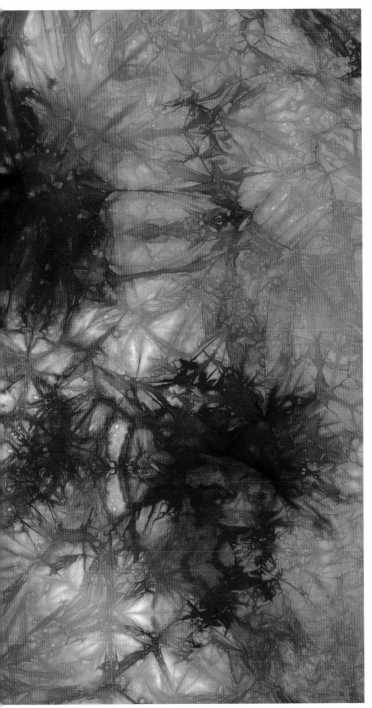

Low-water immersion dyeing produces infinite variety of color combinations, depending on how fabric is manipulated and where colors are poured.

## IMMERSION DYEING

Because immersion dyeing uses a greater amount of water than surface applications, the dyes can bond more quickly to the fiber. In both immersion dyeing methods given here, most of the dye bonds in the first 15 minutes after soda is added, and the process is complete an hour after the soda is added. Surface applications take four to eight hours for the dye to cure. The low-water immersion dye method uses much less water than vat dyeing, which translates as much more efficient for you, less water, less dye and less work. It allows dyers to produce multicolored fabrics, as well as one-color fabrics with an even texture. When I want very even colors for a very large amount of fabric, I consider using the recipe for vat dyeing.

One yard (meter) cotton in each container, following low-water immersion recipe. More dye concentrate in left container results in darker red fabric.

### LOW-WATER IMMERSION DYEING

This method of immersion dyeing is designed to be quick and easy. Use it for cellulose fibers and silks. The results range from fairly even texture to extremely variegated texture. The method uses a low ratio of water to fabric, so salt is unnecessary to the process. There are many, many ways to adapt this low-water immersion dyeing method, some of which are thoroughly detailed in *Color by Accident*.

1. Scour the fabric, if needed, and prepare soda solution, as in Step 1 on page 36.

2. Prepare dye concentrates, as in Step 4 on page 37.

3. Wet fabric with warm water – 1 cup (240 ml) per yard (meter) of fabric. Manipulate the fabric in a container – that is, wrinkle, fold, twist, or tie.

4. Make 1 cup (240 ml) color for each yard (meter) of fabric using dye concentrates and plain water.

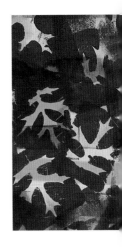

> For light colors     Under 2 tsp (10 ml) dye concentrate
>
> For dark colors     Up to 10 Tbs (150 ml) dye concentrate

Pour one or more colors over the wet fabric. Press out some of the air bubbles and mix. More movement of the fabric will make a more even color.

5. After 5 to 15 minutes, pour 1 cup (240 ml) soda solution per yard (meter) over the fabric. Mix or press to distribute the soda solution through the fabric. More movement of the fabric will make a more even color.

6. Let the dye work for one hour minimum. Press, stir, or turn the fabric once or more often during this time. Again, more movement of the fabric will make a more even color. Options are to press out most of the air bubbles and weight the fabric so it doesn't float in the container, or, after some time has passed, redistribute the wrinkles in the fabric, tie or untie it, stir continuously, or just leave it alone.

7. Remove excess dye by washing, as in Step 8 on page 37. Rinse in warm water, then wash in hot water, 140° F (60° C), with 1/2 tsp (2.5 ml) Synthrapol SP.

## VAT DYEING

This classic recipe for level dyeing (i.e., for even, solid colors), requires a large quantity of water. For 1 lb (455 g) fabric, you will use about 20 lbs (9.1 kilos) of water and 1 lb to 2 lbs (455 g to 910 g) salt, depending on how dark you want your color. The quantities below are given by volume to make measuring easier. If you keep swatches and measure carefully, you can approximately duplicate a color. For more accurate color matching, dye powders should be weighed exactly.

The following recipe allows you to dye 1 lb (455 g) of fabric or about 3 to 4 yards (meters) of cotton.

1. Scour the fabric, if needed, as in Step 1 on page 36.

2. Combine water and salt:

| | |
|---|---|
| Warm water | 2.5 gallons (9.5 l) |
| Salt | 2 - 4 cups (480 - 960 ml) |

3. Add dissolved dye, either concentrate or powders:

| | |
|---|---|
| Dye concentrate | 1 tsp (5 ml) for pale, up to 1 cup (240 ml) for dark |
| Dye powder | 1/4 tsp (1.5 ml) for pale, up to 6 tsp (30 ml) dissolved in 2 cups (480 ml) water for dark |

4. Add wet fabric.

5. Stir for 15 minutes for even color.

6. Add dissolved soda ash (for very dark colors, add more soda):

| | |
|---|---|
| Soda ash | 5 Tbs (75 ml) dissolved in 1 cup (240 ml) water |

7. Stir frequently for one hour. The more you stir, the more even the color will be.

8. Remove excess dye. Rinse in warm water, then wash in hot water, 140° F (60° C), with 1/2 tsp (2.5 ml) Synthrapol SP.

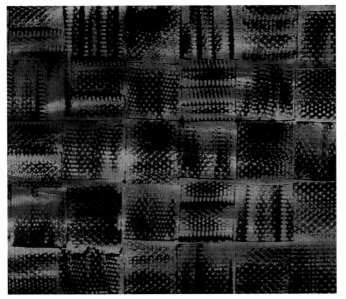

Thick black on smooth sponge roller with impression from paint tray with dots created a black texture on dry fabric. Later, thin colors were painted on background with sponge brush.

## ALTERNATIVE SURFACE APPLICATIONS

Procion®MX dyes can be applied directly to the fabric and cured properly in other ways than the eight-step process that was described in Chapter 2 and that you experimented with in subsequent chapters. Sometimes, your project may require one of these alternatives. You may prefer, for example, not to prepare a dye concentrate, or you may wish to avoid soaking your fabric in soda solution. You may not want to wait for the colors to cure. In some instances, when working with silk only, an alternative method may be best. Other fiber-reactive dyes can be used to immersion dye cellulose fibers and silk, but few of them offer a wide range of colors that will cure at room temperatures, so they require heat or steam equipment for surface applications. Keep in mind that every type of dye requires different conditions for maximum color results and many will not work for painting and printing.

## USING PROCION®MX DYES FOR SILK

Thick colors were brushed on work surface with wide bristle brushes and then dry silk was monoprinted. After colors dried, thick yellow, blue, and red were painted with brushes. Silk was washed and dried, then thick black was applied with needle-tip bottle using the acetic acid recipe for silk.

If you work with silk a lot, consider using this recipe, but note that it cannot be used for cotton. Silk is a special protein fiber because it is a secretion, not a hair growth. This means that silk fiber molecules have reactive groups similar to cellulose fibers. For silks and wool, acid – rather than alkali – can be used as the dye assistant with Procion®MX dyes. Using acid allows you to skip soaking the fabric in soda solution. You can add acid directly to the colors you mix, then paint or print. Given time, soda and moisture combine to damage silk fibers, so this alternative recipe is a good one to consider.

### STEP 1    PREPARE FABRIC

Prepare as described in Step 1 on page 36. Silk often contains silk worm gum, and if any is left in the fabric, it will show after the silk is dyed. Silk is de-gummed at 180° F (82° C), so do not worry about using hot water. Silk is sensitive, however, to sudden drops in temperature, so avoid putting silk directly from hot to cold water.

### STEP 2    PREPARE PRINT PASTE

Prepare as described in Step 2 on page 36. Add 2 tsp (10 ml) of 56 percent acetic acid per quart. Citric acid crystals may be substituted for the acetic acid – 4 tsp (20 ml) per quart. If very fine-line definition is needed in your paint or print project, you may wish to use sodium alginate F, which is a low-viscosity, high-solids thickener sometimes used for silk, instead of sodium alginate SH.

## STEP 3   PREPARE UREA WATER

Prepare urea water to thin print paste to desired consistency, as in Step 3 on page 36. Add acetic or citric acid to the urea water in the same proportion, to maintain the concentration of acid when you add it to the print paste.

## STEP 4   PREPARE DYE CONCENTRATES

Prepare colors for use following Step 4 on page 37. Add acetic or citric acid in the same portion.

## STEP 5   PREPARE COLORS

Combine dye stock and print paste and urea water to the desired consistency, color and value, following Step 5 on page 37.

## STEP 6   APPLY COLORS

Apply the dye mixture to the treated fabric using any surface design technique you like: brush, stamp, roller, sponge, wood block, silk screen, and many more.

## STEP 7   CURE FABRIC

Cure by letting the dyes bond with the fiber at room temperature, maintaining a slight amount of moisture. For citric acid cure for 12 - 24 hours. For acetic acid cure 24 - 48 hours.

## STEP 8   WASH OUT EXCESS DYE

Wash out dye and test the fabric for color fastness, following Step 8 on page 37.

### ADD ALKALI

For this method, you do not pre-soak the fabric in soda solution, but rather add alkali to the colors. Because soda ash causes the dye to react and dramatically shortens the shelf life of the color from four or more days to about an hour, a milder mix of soda ash and baking soda is recommended for this method. Because the alkali mix is milder, the dye should be allowed to cure for a longer time. I use this method if I plan to apply the dye very quickly and have a lot of fabric to cover. After 4 hours, the dye/soda mixture will appear to be the same value, but after washing the fabric, you will see a lot more color loss than you would using fresh dye and alkali mix.

1. Make a dry mix of alkali. Stir thoroughly and store airtight until ready to use.

    Four parts sodium bicarbonate (baking soda)

    One part sodium carbonate (soda ash)

2. When ready to print or paint, combine and use within 4 hours:

    1 tsp (5 ml) dry alkali mix

    1 cup (240 ml) color (dye concentrate mixed with print paste and/or urea water)

3. Cure, with a slight amount of moisture, for 24 hours at room temperature.

4. Wash out excess dye.

### STEAM THE FABRIC

In some cases, you may not wish to cure the fabric for 4 to 8 hours. To cut curing time, you can steam the fabric. You can either buy a professional steamer or make one with a large kettle. It should allow the heat to flow through all the layers of the fabric without depositing moisture on the fabric. If the steam is too moist, it will cause the transfer of color through the layers anyway. If the steam is too hot or is applied for too long, it can cook the print paste, making it difficult to wash out. With large quantities of fabric, a practical approach is to have it steamed professionally.

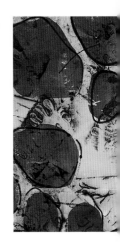

1. Do not soak the fabric in the soda solution.

2. Combine:

> 1 tsp (5 ml) baking soda (sodium bicarbonate)
>
> 1 cup (240 ml) color (dye concentrate mixed with print paste and/or urea water)

Store refrigerated and use within three days.

3. Paint or print.

4. Let the fabric dry.

5. Steam for 10 to 15 minutes, rolled in clean paper or fabric so that no dyed parts touch, to prevent the transfer of colors.

6. Wash out excess dye.

# QUESTIONS & ANSWERS

You have read the text, done all the exercises, and followed some of the suggestions and you still have questions? I have sorted and answered some of the most frequently asked questions here, hoping to address most of yours. Keep in mind that something new always seems more difficult. Most of your confusion, particularly about what works and why, will be answered by your own experience and practice.

Thin colors were sprayed onto dry fabric through a grid with circular holes, then thick black was printed with x-shaped sponge.

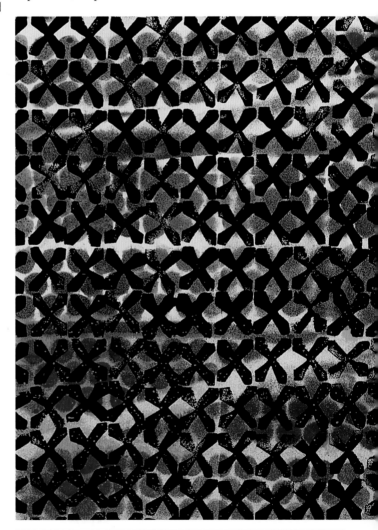

The most important question comes first. If you can remember the answer, you don't need this book anymore.

**What happened to make the colors look lighter than I expected?** Remember that transparent colors look much darker when wet than dry. If you have applied more dye than the fabric can absorb, the fabric will look lighter after it is washed, but as a general rule, *the way the fabric looks after it is painted and dry should be very close to the way it looks when it is washed and dried.* If not, check for the following possibilities:

• Was a less reactive dye used, not Procion®MX?

• Was pure sodium carbonate used?

• Was the soda solution mixed the right strength?

• Was the soda solution washed out by the rain or by a water spray in the spin cycle of the washer?

• Is the fabric 100 percent cellulose fiber or 100 percent silk?

• Is the fabric loose-weave or very thin?

• Was the dye powder dissolved in water over 95° F (35° C)?

• Was the dye powder stored too long, too warm, or too damp?

• Was the dye concentrate stored too long or too warm?

• Was the dye concentrate mixed with too much print paste and/or urea water?

• Were colors painted over too many layers of dye and print paste?

• Did you cure the fabrics at room temperature?

• Did the fabric dry before all the dye could fix?

Notched sponge brushes make red checkerboard. When those marks were almost dry, rollers with thick violet and tan were rolled across fabric.

## PRODUCTS

**What is the difference between dye and paint?** Fabric paints and inks are often referred to as dyes because they color the fabric. However, a distinction should be made between them because of how they work. Paints and inks are ground pigments that must contain a *binder* to make the pigment adhere to the fiber. The binder is often a resin-like substance that requires heat treatment and usually adds a stiffness to the surface of the fabric, particularly in areas of intense color. Dyes have a chemical bond with the fibers that does not change the hand of the fabric. Fiber-reactive dyes have an electron bond which is very strong, allowing the fabric to withstand repeated washings and strong light. Other types of dye link with the fiber in various ways and vary in strength accordingly.

I consider paints and inks an important option for embellishing the fabric after it is dyed and washed. Using fabric paint is a good way to add light areas to dark fabric, or metallic highlights to the design. There are many brands, new ones appearing all the time. They vary tremendously in their ability to stick to the fabric and other characteristics – their qualities can only be judged by trial. Keep in mind the function of the fabric and how often it will be washed. When choosing and testing paints and inks for fabric, be sure to consider the following: light fastness, wash fastness, rub fastness, how they feel and look when stitched, and the overall texture and drape of the fabric.

### What ecological considerations are there in using and disposing of Procion®MX dyes and related chemicals?

In surface applications of dye, a very small amount of dye is used and about 90 percent of it is attached to the fibers when the correct curing is done. Any dye that does not react with the fiber is inert or no longer reactive, because it has bonded with water before dyeing or during the wash-out process. The sodium carbonate used in the dye process is also in the laundry detergents we use. It is a natural product of the earth, and it should be disposed of in the same way as your laundry products. Synthrapol is also similar to many laundry products and can be handled accordingly. Urea is a moisturizing agent found in many cosmetics. Sodium alginate is a protein extracted from seaweed and is harmless.

### Can I paint and print on wool with Procion®MX dyes?

Wool requires acid for fiber-reactive dyes to bond. Procion®MX dyes can be formulated with acid to work with wool. There are many things to consider for dyeing wool, and I would recommend that you consider using one of the acid dyes that are made for wool before you begin.

### Is there a product that will cut down on the work of washing out excess dyes from fabric? Synthrapol SP is designed to do just that. The letters "SP" stand for "soaping Procion." It gets into the fibers and works to release any unreacted dye. Hot water and agitation of the fabric increase the release of unreacted dye. I use Synthrapol SP in each wash until all the unreacted dye is out. After that, I use regular laundry detergent.

**Should I use Retayne or similar products for washing my dyed fabrics?** Retayne is a retention agent designed for direct dyes that are not wash fast. It will also react with fiber-reactive dyes. Retention products each work at a particular temperature, making the molecules larger, trapping the dye within the fibers, and increasing their wet-fastness. After one is used, the fabric should not be washed in hot water, because this will release trapped dye molecules.

A retention agent is not necessary with Procion®MX dyes because they produce a bond between the fiber and the dye that is not water-soluble. The excess dye needs to be washed away; then the fabric is ready to use. In fact, if such a product were used with Procion®MX dye, some of the unreacted dye may be trapped on the fiber and released later when it is washed in hot water, possibly staining the fabric.

**Can I use washing soda from the grocery store in place of soda ash?** No, washing soda sold as a laundry product is of undetermined strength and has additives such as bleach and perfume, which could influence the results you get with the dye process. Sodium carbonate is the chemical required, and the purer the form used, the more predictable the results. The same is true of water softeners from the grocery store if used in place of metaphos in the print paste.

**Why don't you use gutta as a resist?** Gutta is a general term used for many products that are used for holding the flow of dyes within the lines where it is painted. Some of them are water-soluble, others are not. They are most often used for silk scarf painting with thin dyes. Many of them do not penetrate heavier weaves of fabric and do not resist the dye if it is painted over the gutta.

Clear print paste painted on silk with thickened colors blended on top. Fine lines were painted on dry fabric.

**Can I use powdered Procion®MX dyes without making dye concentrates?** You may want to use powdered dyes instead of dye concentrate for your painting and printing. Though this method is popular with some dyers, it is not one I recommend. I find it more trouble to measure the powder accurately than it is worth. For this method, follow all the steps on page 36 - 37, but skip Step 4. Instead, wearing a dust mask, measure the dry powder directly into 1 cup (240 ml) print paste. If it doesn't dissolve easily, try stirring a small amount of warm water into the powder.

> For pale colors   1/2 tsp (2.5 ml) or less dye powder
>
> For dark colors   Up to 6 tsp (30 ml) dye powder

Store refrigerated up to five days, as long there is no contamination with soda ash.

**What if I cannot find Procion®MX dyes where I live?**
Procion®MX dyes were originally formulated for industrial use, and our ability to get the products we need for studio work are dependent on that fact. The dye suppliers for artists buy and repackage products from the chemical industry in quantities we can use during their shelf life.

We live in a global marketplace. Procion®MX dyes have been manufactured by several different companies over the years and in different countries around the world. You might live in the country of manufacture, and not be able to buy it there. When I buy dye, it has been made in one country and sold to a distributor in another country before being shipped to me in Oregon from another state in the United States.

**Will I always be able to find Procion®MX dyes?** Many producers and manufacturers depend on using particular chemicals like Procion®MX dyes, and they will be in demand for a long time. There may be completely new dyes someday that will work with cellulose and silk under the same conditions as Procion®MX dyes, but availability of chemicals depends on legislation and approval by government agencies in addition to perceived demand by suppliers. There are many dyes that work well and easily in immersion dyeing conditions, some requiring hotter temperatures, but they are not as simple to use for surface applications on fabric because their heat and moisture requirements are higher than room temperature. When there is a product that is simpler and cheaper to paint on fabric than Procion®MX, I will be using it, no matter what it is named.

**Can I buy dye already mixed with water to avoid mixing powders?** Procion®MX dyes are not sold as liquids because at temperatures above 70° F (21° C) they will react with water over time and lose their strength. Dyes sold as a liquid are not as reactive as Procion®MX dyes.

## Can I use other fiber-reactive dyes with these

**recipes?** ®Cibacron F dyes, also referred to by some suppliers as Sabracron dyes, are less reactive than Procion® MX dyes, so they react more slowly with the fabric and can be stored longer when mixed with water. Recipes and applications are similar to those designed for Procion® MX dye, but curing times are twice as long, that is 12 to 48 hours. They require warmer temperatures over a broader range: 105° F to 120° F (40° C to 50° C), so some colors will work acceptably at room temperature following these recipes and others will not. There are fewer single-chemical colors in ®Cibacron F dyes than in Procion® MX dyes.

Cotton was monoprinted, then painted, masked and painted again.

Procion® H dyes are very much less reactive than Procion® MX dyes, so they can be stored longer in solution and are often sold in liquid form. Their slower reactivity also means that they will not work without stronger alkali, heat and/or more time to make them bond with the fibers. They require temperatures of 170° F to 80° F (77° C to 82° C) for curing. They should not be used for painting or printing without steaming equipment. They will not work with the recipes in this book.

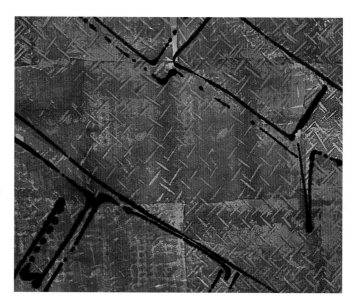

Roller impression picked up from the paint tray on dry fabric. Lines of thick black were drawn over wet colors.

## PROCESS

**If I have refrigerated the dye stock, should I warm it to room temperature before I paint or print?** Do not try to heat the dyes; temperatures over about 100° F (38° C) will damage them. If you combine the dye stock with print paste and urea water that have been stored at room temperature, the mixture is warmed up considerably when you mix them with cold dye concentrate. In any case, when the color is put on the fabric in a thin layer in a warm room, it gets up to room temperature fairly quickly. The temperature during the cure time is the essential element.

**If I don't remember whether or not I put the fabric in soda, do I have to wash it before I put it in soda again?** No, putting it in the soda solution will not change the concentration of the alkali. Soak the fabric in your soda solution (again) whenever you are in doubt.

**Suppose I painted my fabric and then realize that I forgot to put it in soda. What should I do?** If you put it in a soda solution after you paint, much of the dye will float off and smear all over the fabric. If you spray soda solution on, it will blur. I suggest washing your fabric thoroughly and starting over with what is left. You will be amazed how much dye sticks when there is no soda, but that dye is not bonded. It is only staining the fabric and is not fast to light or washing.

**I am making a piece for the wall. Why do I have to wash my dyed fabric?** One reason to use dye is to maintain the texture and weight of the fabric; the unfixed dye and chemicals fill and cover the weave of the fabric until it is washed. Silk, for example, will not have the glow or sheen associated with it if the surface is covered. Also, the sodium alginate in the print paste is pure protein, and in combination with urea, which attracts moisture, the fabric will look dull and possibly get moldy if not washed out. Most importantly, the excess dye that has not reacted with the fiber molecules will have poor light fastness and can bleed if in contact with moisture.

**Why did the white areas of my design become tinted during washing?** This happens when you move to hot water too suddenly in the washout process, before the soda has been completely removed. Even though the dye is no longer reactive, having bonded either with the fiber or the water in the dyeing process, those molecules not bonded to the fiber circulate in the wash water and can act as direct dyes if any alkali is present. Direct dyes sit between the fibers and have very poor wash-fastness. If the staining is not too bad, several hot washes with Synthrapol SP may wash out some color. Silk requires the most care in washing because it stains more easily than cotton. It will hold a lot of color even without acid or alkali, although those colors will have poor wash-fastness.

**Why does silk work with alkali or acid recipes?** Silk is a protein fiber, but it does not have the same molecular make up as wool or other furs, which require acid for dyeing. Its structure has a site with which the Procion®MX dyes can bond using either alkali or acid. Alkali can damage silk fibers if it remains moist for a long time, however, you will not have any problems with deterioration of the silk fibers if you store the silk soaked in soda solution and keep it 100 percent dry. To be safe, use dry, soda-soaked silk within a month, and make sure it is washed soon after the dye has cured, whether painted, printed, or immersion dyed.

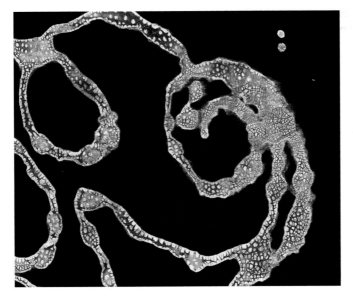

White cotton was crumpled tightly and dyed orange in low-water immersion dyebath. It was washed, dried, soda-soaked, dried again and painted with hot potato dextrin from a squeeze bottle. After the dextrin dried, thick black was rolled over all.

# TECHNIQUES

**Why is the dye bleeding out beyond my pencil line as I paint?** Control of the flow of the colors takes practice. The dye concentrate and print paste need to be mixed to the consistency appropriate to the mark you want to make and the tool you use. There are some things to keep in mind that might increase your control.

• After you wash the brush, squeeze out excess water with a towel.

• Work on dry fabric; the line will spread more if the fabric is wet.

• Too much dye concentrate in medium or thin print paste makes the mixture too runny. If you want to use double-strength color, start with thick print paste.

• Even when the color is extra-thick, if it is mounded on heavily, it will flatten and spread.

• When working with medium or thin color, be ready to blot it with a paper towel to control its flow.

**How many layers of color can I paint on top of each other?** The answer depends on how dark the colors are and how thick you use them. The print paste itself slightly resists the penetration of dye into fibers. One thick layer will resist and dilute the next layer of color considerably. If the first layer is navy blue, a subsequent layer of yellow will not have much visual impact. If layers of thick pale colors are applied first, then black is painted over it, the fabric will look black before it is washed, but not after; it will be gray. The dye can penetrate colors that were mixed with thin or medium-thin print paste more easily. The first color applied to the fabric penetrates the most and will show through any other color. Practice will help you predict the final color of the fabric. After I apply several layers of color, I sometimes want to see what I have, so I wash and dry it. Then, if I want to apply more color, I soak it in soda solution again and get to work.

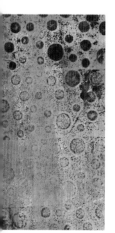

**Can I iron the fabric after it has been painted but not washed?** Allow time for the fabric to cure and dry first. If you don't wait, the dyes won't have their fullest color. If the fabric has dried with wrinkles and lumps because it was not stretched and you want to work on flat fabric, iron it with a warm iron, not hot. Remember that sodium alginate is a protein and it can be hard to wash out if it has been heated too much.

**How can I make colors turn out exactly the same each time?** With paint and print applications this is practically impossible. Even if you measure the dye powders by weight and use them with exactly the same amount of print paste, measured by weight, the density of color will vary with every brush stroke or stamp mark you make. The beauty of hand-produced textiles is their individuality, not their uniformity.

**When should I spread print paste on the fabric before I paint?** Print paste acts as a slight resist when color is painted or printed over it, so I only use this technique when I want a surface that allows me to spread the color evenly and smoothly, blending a large area. This is very difficult to do on dry fabric or fabric that is wet with soda solution. Print paste wets the fabric, and allows you to move some of the color around on it. If there is an area of the design that I wish to be very dark, I paint or print it first, let it cure, and then put print paste over it.

**What causes patches of washed-out colors where I have applied a lot of dye?** When soda solution is on the fabric and a lot of dye is applied in one place, whether thick or thin, the liquid may dilute the soda solution so that it is not concentrated enough to fix the dyes in that spot. I usually brush or blot away any blobs of excess dye before I leave it to cure, in order to minimize this effect.

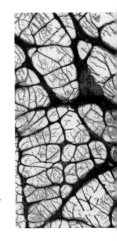

**Why do colors appear lighter than I expect when I paint on wet soda-soaked fabric?** The colors spread out when you work on wet fabric; they are not as concentrated as they would be when they stay where you put them. Also, the colors are diluted by the moisture in the soda solution. If I want very dark colors on wet fabric, I use double-strength colors to compensate for all the liquid in the fabric.

**How long do I have to wait before I can paint over a layer of color without smearing it?** That depends on how quickly it is drying and what you plan to do. Using a heavy stroke over partly dry color may smear it away from where it was placed. If you wait until the area first painted is almost dry to the touch and paint lightly over it, working towards the color and not away from it, you can proceed without too much smearing. Block printing may pick up some of the color that was first put down and place it on the next place you print. That, however, may give you exactly the hand-painted effect you want.

# glossary

**Acetic acid, 56 percent:** Concentrated liquid acid eleven times the strength of vinegar, used with Procion®MX dyes for silk and wool.

**Auxiliary chemicals:** Products that are used in dyeing to aid the processes.

**Baking soda:** Sodium bicarbonate. Weaker alkali than soda ash, sometimes used in fixing surface applications of fiber-reactive dyes.

Thin red and blue sprayed on gently wrinkled dry cotton.

**Binder:** Chemical used in fabric paints and inks to make ground pigments in them adhere to surface of fabric.

**Brights:** Brushes that have short bristles in flat, rectangular shape.

**Causticize:** Treatment of cellulose fabrics with caustic alkali solution that improves color yield of dyes. It is similar in concept to mercerizing but with slightly different results in the hand of the fabric.

**Cellulose fiber:** Any fiber produced by plants; a fiber having a chemical structure that can react with fiber-reactive dye molecules.

**Citric acid:** Crystal-form acid that can replace acetic acid for use with Procion®MX dyes.

**Color fastness:** Ability of dyed cloth to hold color in different conditions. When washed in water, fastness of a color is measured on a scale of 1 to 5 (high). When it is exposed to light, fastness is measured on a scale of 1 to 8 (high). Colors on fabric can also be described in terms of rub fastness, depending on how easily they rub off surface.

**Color Index:** Reference that categorizes dyes by their trade names and color numbers. All dyes of same type and color are given the same Color Index number so equivalents can be found.

**Complementary colors:** Colors directly opposite each other on color wheel: red and green, yellow and violet, blue and orange.

**Curing:** Fixation stage of dye process when dye bonds with fiber molecules.

**Dextrin:** Substance found in many foods. A long chain of glucose units (sugars) made from starch in vegetables. It is water-soluble and very sticky and can be used as adhesive, as sizing, and as resist. Potato dextrin is also called British gum.

**Dye site:** Location on fiber where chemical reaction takes place. There are more dye sites for fiber-reactive dyes on cotton than on silk.

**Direct dye:** Dye for cellulose fabrics with weak chemical bonds between dye and fiber, having only poor to fair wash fastness.

**Discharge:** To remove color on fabric by destroying the dye with a chemical, leaving a lighter color where the product was applied. Chlorine bleach, which is often used as a discharge chemical for dyed cotton, should be neutralized soon after dye discharge to stop the chemical process that eventually destroys the fibers.

**Dye assistant:** Chemical used to create conditions for dye reaction; for example soda ash for Procion®MX dyes on cotton; also called **dye activator.**

**Dye concentrate:** Solution of dye in water. Adding urea to dye concentrate allows more dye powder to dissolve, resulting in stronger colors.

**Fat quarter:** Yard (meter) of fabric divided vertically and horizontally into four equal pieces; measures approximately 18″ x 22″ (45 x 55 cm), depending on width of fabric.

**Fiber-reactive dyes:** Synthetic dyes that react with fiber to create strong chemical bond. They are used with cellulose fibers, silk, and wool. They require alkali or acid as fixative.

**Gradation:** Gradual change from one color or value to another.

**Greige:** Fabric in untreated condition, as it comes from loom.

**Hand:** Weight, texture, and drape of fabric; how it feels to touch.

**Hue:** Name of color. Property of colors by which they can be perceived as ranging from red through yellow, green, and blue, as determined by dominant wavelength of light.

**Immersion dyeing:** Application of dyes with large ratio of water to dye. For example, when Procion®MX dyes are used in a dye-bath with soda ash, standard recipe calls for weight of water to be 20 times weight of fabric.

**Intensity:** Degree of brightness or purity of color. Also **chroma, saturation.**

**Light-sensitive emulsion:** Mixture of chemicals that can be spread on silk screens and exposed to light to create design from positive image. Also called **photo-sensitive emulsion.**

**Low-water immersion dyeing:** Similar to **immersion dyeing,** but using about 20 percent of water and no salt.

**Ludigol:** Trade name for sodium salt of m-nitrobenzene sulfonic acid, or resist salts L. It is used in some applications of fiber-reactive dyes, because it may increase dye fixation during curing.

**Mercerize:** Treatment for cotton with caustic soda, giving fiber greater strength, luster, and affinity to dyes.

**Metaphos:** Chemical used in print paste when sodium alginate is used as thickener to make alginate flow more smoothly. Also used as water softener: sodium hexametaphosphate.

**Migrate:** Spreading of dye to areas not painted.

**Needle-tip bottle:** Plastic bottle top with long narrow point and very fine hole.

**Pigment:** Insoluble color-producing components of paints and inks, requiring **binder** to make pigments adhere to fibers.

**Primary colors:** Three basic colors from which all others are theoretically derived. For dyers, they are red, blue, and yellow.

**Print paste:** Mixture of chemicals and water used in direct applications of dyes. It can be mixed thin, like water, or thick, like a paste or gel.

**Procion®:** Trade name for one of many fiber-reactive dyes with their own particular chemical characteristics. Procion®H dyes are much less reactive and require more heat or alkali to make them work than Procion®MX dyes.

**Registration:** Process of matching parts of a pattern together, such as printing design using several different silk screen designs in same place.

**Repeat:** Repetition of design element in continuing geometric relationship. Repeat may be exact or approximate, creating rhythm.

**Resist:** Anything used to prevent penetration of dye into fiber, such as binding the fabric tightly or covering an area of fabric with masking tape, wax, or starch pastes. Some resists are suitable for immersion, some only for surface applications.

**Rounds:** Brushes with bristles that make round pointed shape.

**Scour:** Wash fabric to remove anything that might interfere with dye process.

**Secondary color:** Color produced when two primary colors are combined in any amounts. Red and yellow result in orange, red and blue result in violet, and blue and yellow result in green.

**Single-chemical color:** Dye color that is not a mixture of various chemicals. Also referred to as **self-color.**

**Sizing:** Starch or other stiffener used in finishing fabric to protect fibers and improve its appearance. Sizing resists penetration of dye into fibers.

**Soda ash:** 100 percent sodium carbonate, the alkali used for fixing fiber-reactive dyes, often referred to as washing soda. Washing soda sold at grocery stores may not be pure 100 percent sodium carbonate.

**Sodium alginate SH:** Thickener used in print paste for applying dye to surface of fabric. It is used for both cotton and silk. Less is needed than is the case with sodium alginate F, which has smaller grains that do not swell up as much.

**Surfactant:** Surface active agent in many detergents which keeps chemicals and other particles in suspension in water.

**Synthrapol SP:** Concentrated surface active agent used with fiber-reactive dyes to prewash fabric and wash out unreacted dye. It acts as surfactant, keeping unreacted dye in suspension and lessening chance of color transfer.

**Tencel®:** Registered product of viscose rayon that is produced using wood pulp. It is woven to look and feel like cotton or silk.

**Transparent:** Capable of being seen through. With dyes, one color over another will result in color that is combination of both.

**Urea:** Chemically formulated granules used in surface applications of Procion® MX dyes to keep fiber slightly moist, which is required for maximum dye reaction.

**Value:** Degree of lightness or darkness of a color.

**Vat dyeing:** Same as **immersion dyeing** with a 20 to 1 water to fabric ratio.

**Viscose rayon:** Rayon made from wood fibers with very high affinity for Procion® MX dyes. Rayon has some of characteristics of cotton and can be produced to have very high luster. Some fabrics named rayon are made with synthetic fibers and will not accept fiber-reactive dyes.

**Yorker cap:** Pointed plastic bottle top with small cap. It can have a pin hole or be cut for larger hole.

# sources

*Stay current on suppliers and prices by watching magazine advertising and using the Internet.*

Codes for products: 1 – fabric, 2 – MX dyes, 3 – tools/supplies, 4 – books

Patterns were made by rolling dark colors over fabric with a grid under it. Later, rust and blue were rolled over.

# USA

**Aljo Manufacturing Co.**
81-83 Franklin Street
New York, NY 10013
Tel: 212-966-4046
Fax: 212-274-9616
2, 3

**Clearsnap, Inc.**
Box 98
Anacortes, WA 98221
Tel: 800-448-4862, 360-293-6634
Fax: 360-293-6699
www.clearsnap.com
3; also foam blocks and sheets

**Color Creek-Fiber Art**
5520 Lake Otis Parkway #104
Anchorage, AK 99507
Tel: 907-344-7967
www.color-creek.com
1, 2, 3, 4

**Daniel Smith**
P.O. Box 84268
Seattle, WA 98124-5568
Tel: 800-426-6740
Fax: 800-238-4065
www.danielsmith.com
3

**Dharma Trading Company**
P.O. Box 150916
San Rafael, CA 94915
Tel: 800-542-5227, 415-456-7657
Fax: 415-456-8747
www.dharmatrading.com
1, 2, 3, 4

**Dick Blick**
P.O. Box 1267
Galesburg, IL 61402
Tel: 800-828-4548, 309-343-6181
Fax: 800-621-8293
www.dickblick.com
3

**Earth Guild**
33 Hayward Street
Asheville, NC 28801
Tel: 800-327-8448, 828-255-7818
Fax: 828-255-8593
www.earthguild.com
1, 2, 3, 4

**Exotic Silks**
1959 B Leghorn
Mountain View, CA 94043
Tel: 800-854-7455 US,
    800-345-7455 CA
Fax: 650-965-0712
www.exoticsilks.com
1

**Midwest Sign &
Screen Printing Supply**
5035 NW Front Street
Portland, OR 97210
Tel: 503-224-1400, 800-228-0596
Fax: 800-278-0596
www.midwestsignandscreen.com
3

**Nasco Arts and Crafts**
910 Janesville Avenue
Fort Atkinson, WI 53538
Tel: 800-558-9595
Fax: 920-563-8296
www.nascofa.com
3

**PRO Chemical and Dye**
P.O. Box 14
Somerset, MA 02726
Tel: 800-228-9393, 508-676-3838
Fax: 508-676-3980
www.prochemical.com
1, 2, 3, 4

**Silkpaint Corporation**
P.O. Box 18
Waldron, MO 64092-0018
Tel: 800-563-0074, 816-891-7774
Fax: 816-891-7775
www.silkpaint.com
3, resist and air pen

**Standard Dyes, Inc.**
P.O. Box 2808
High Point, NC 27261
Tel: 800-859-1240, 336-841-5468
Fax: 336-841-5463
www.standarddyes.com
2, 3

**Testfabrics, Inc.**
P.O. Box 26
West Pittston, PA 18643
Tel: 570-603-0432
Fax: 570-603-0433
www.testfabrics.com
1

**Wildfiber**
1453-e 14th Street
Santa Monica, CA 90404
Tel: 800-382-7067, 310-458-2748
Fax: 310-458-9000
www.wildfiber.com
1, 2, 3, 4

# INTERNATIONAL

**CCG Industries**
33 Crowhurst Street
Box 9523, Newmarket
Auckland, New Zealand
Tel: 64-9-524-9758
Fax: 64-9-522-0635
C.C.G.@extra.co.nz
2, 3

**Craft Supplies**
31 Gurney Road
Belmont, Lower Hutt
New Zealand
Tel/Fax: 64-4-565-0544
www.dianaparkes.co.nz
1, 2, 3, 4

**Galerie Smend**
Mainzer Strasse 31, Köln
50678 Germany
Tel: 69-221-312-0474
Fax: 69-221-932-0718
www.smend.de
1, 2, 3, 4

**George Weil & Fibrecrafts**
Old Portsmouth Road
Peasmarsh, Guilford, Surrey
GU3 1LZ England
Tel: 44-1483-565-800
Fax: 44-1483-565-807
sales@georgeweil.co.uk
2, 3

**G&S Dye Ltd.**
300 Steelcase Rd. W., Unit #19
Markham, Ontario
L3R 2W2 Canada
Tel: 800-596-0550, 416-596-0550
Fax: 416-596-0493
www.gsdye.com
2, 3

**Kaleidoscope,
Creative Inspirations**
5 Pendicle Road
Beardsen, Glasgow
G61 1PU United Kingdom
Tel: 44-141-942-8511
Fax: 44-141-942-8511
2, 4

**Kraftkolour**
242 High Street
Northcote, Victoria
3070 Australia
Tel: 61-3-9482-9234
Fax: 61-3-9482-9279
kkolour@vegas.com.au
2, 3

**Maiwa Handprints, Ltd.**
#6-16666 Johnston Street
Vancouver, BC V6H 3S2 Canada
Tel: 604-669-3939
Fax: 604-669-3939
www.maiwa.com
2, 3, 4

**Midland Dykem Ltd.**
71 Paget Road
Leicester
LE3 5HN United Kingdom
Tel: 44-1533-624-975
Fax: 44-1533-627-425
2

**Multicraft Manufacturing Ltd.**
137 Eban Avenue, Auckland
1309 New Zealand
Tel: 64-9-480-5456
Fax: 64-9-418-1546
2

**Quilt und Art**
Postfach 1254
Mühlheim/Main
63152 Germany
Tel: 49-6108-73060
Fax: 49-6108-709-949
www.quiltundart.de
1, 2, 3

**Tillia Dyes**
62 Cook Drive, Whitianga
2856 New Zealand
Tel: 64-7-866-4939
1, 2, 3, 4

**Whaleys (Bradford) Ltd.**
Harris Court, Great Horton
Bradford, West Yorkshire
BD7 4EQ United Kingdom
Tel: 44-1274-576-718
Fax: 44-1274-521-309
www.whaleys.co.uk
1

**Zijdelings**
Korte Tunistraat 13
Tilburg
5038 SJ Netherlands
Tel: 31-13-580-0343
Fax: 31-13-580-0345
www.zijdelings.com
1, 2, 3

JEROME HART

First, Ann learned to sew, then she learned to dye fabric. In between, she earned a BA in Literature from Stanford University and an MA in Geography from the University of Oregon, married Jim, worked in Peace Corps Peru, and taught school in the US. By now, Ann has been putting dye on fabric for over 25 years. Her years of experimentation have led to mountains of hand-dyed fabric and hundreds of one-of-a-kind quilts. Since she wrote *Dye Painting!,* Ann has continued to explore even more variations that work best with Procion®MX dyes. She has also enjoyed giving workshops all over the world, seeing first-hand how people learn and develop their skills with dyes. *Color by Accident: Low-Water Immersion Dyeing,* describes a quick and easy method to create richly textured fabrics. The popularity of that book pushed her to write its companion book, *Color by Design: Paint and Print with Dye,* a very complete manual of techniques for surface design with the same dyes. In her book, *The Quilter's Book of Design,* you can see some of Ann's quilts, made exclusively with her hand-dyed fabrics. If Ann isn't at home in Oregon dyeing fabric or making quilts, you may run into her in a workshop in the US or Europe, doing the same thing, or even more likely, somewhere on the road or trail with Jim and one or both of their sons, Scott and Tod.

*"You have opened up an entirely new way of thinking and working in fabric surface design, and thus have changed me forever as both artist and teacher. I found you to be a superb instructor, informative, knowledgeable, motivational, curious, supportive, organized, helpful, congenial. I am deeply grateful to have had the opportunity to benefit from your wonderful teaching." —Sharon Kesterson Bollen, Fine Arts Professor, College of Mount St. Joseph, Ohio*

*Color by Design: Paint
and Print with Dye*
$29.95
168 pages
ISBN # 0-9656776-1-3

*Color by Accident: Low-Water
Immersion Dyeing*
$24.95
96 pages
ISBN# 0-9656776-0-5

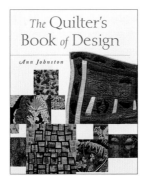

*The Quilter's Book of Design*
$27.95
146 pages
ISBN# 0-8442-2660-2

*Order books from
Ann Johnston at*
PO Box 388
Ashland, OH 44805
Tel: 800-247-6553
Fax: 419-281-6883

order@bookmaster.com

*For workshop and lecture
information contact*
Ann Johnston
P.O. Box 944
Lake Oswego, OR 97034

www.annjohnston.net

Inside back cover:
Large washers and
plastic grids were
used for impressions
on rollers, making
repeat images.